Asian Cookbook

Enjoy Delicious Asian
Cooking with over 90 Delicious
Asian Recipes

By
BookSumo Press
All rights reserved

Published by
http://www.booksumo.com

LEGAL NOTES

All Rights Reserved. No Part Of This Book May Be Reproduced Or Transmitted In Any Form Or By Any Means. Photocopying, Posting Online, And / Or Digital Copying Is Strictly Prohibited Unless Written Permission Is Granted By The Book's Publishing Company. Limited Use Of The Book's Text Is Permitted For Use In Reviews Written For The Public.

Table of Contents

Korean BBQ Short Ribs: Gal-Bi 9

Spicy Tofu Salad 10

Korean Kimchee Squats 11

Korean Carrot Salad 12

Spicy Red Pepper Cucumbers 13

Korean Salad with Sesame Dressing 14

Korean Cucumber Salad 15

Kimchee Jun: Kimchee Pancakes 16

Jap Chae: Glass Noodles 17

Kongnamool: Korean Soybean Sprouts 18

Bulgogi: Korean Chicken Stir Fry 19

Red Pepper Potatoes 20

Korean Fiddleheads 21

Korean Crab Cakes 22

Korean Cashew Hummus 23

Bibimbap: Korean Vegetable Hot Pot 24

Korean Vegetables 25

Korean Whole Chicken 26

Korean Pizzas 27

Soon Du Bu Jigae: Tofu Stew 28

Chicken Stew Korean 29

Tuna and Rice: Chompchae Deopbap 30

Kalbi Jim: Korean Ribs II 31

Korean Burritos 32

Korean Curry 33

Yaki Mandu: Korean Egg Rolls 34

Korean Egg Rolls II 35

How to Make Kimchee 36

Chap Chee Noodles 37

Korean Sushi 38

Classical Pad Thai Noodles I 39

Galbi: Korean Short Ribs III 40

Easy Hummus Thai Style 41

Fresh Thai Pesto 42

Curry Thai Chicken with Pineapple 43

Classical Pad Thai Noodles II 44

Brown Rice Vegetable Soup 45

How to Make Peanut Sauce 46

Thai Style Broccoli Mix 47

Thai Orange Chicken 48

Thai BBQ Chicken 49

Thai Cucumber Soup 50

Thai Chicken Curry 51

Charong's Ginger Soup 52

Thai Veggie Soup 53

Thai Chicken Curry II 54

Classical Shrimp In Thailand 55

Thai Chicken Patties 56

Homemade Thai Pizzas 57

Fresh Basil Chicken 58

Easy Coconut Soup II 59

Spicy Thai Pasta 60

Fried Chicken from Thailand 61

Spicy Lime Shrimp 62

Honey Chili and Peanut Noodles 64

Thai Sweet Short Grain 65

Thai Lunch Box: Peanut, Jalapeno, and Cucumber Salad 66

Classical Peanut Sauce II 67

Thai Mango Curry Chicken and Rice 68

Vietnamese Spring Rolls 69

Spicy Thai Cabbage and Shrimp 70

Classical Pad Thai Noodles III 71

Vietnamese Chicken Meatballs 72

Vietnamese Lamb Chops 73

Vietnamese Chicken Salad 74

Vietnamese Stir-Fry 75

Vietnamese Tofu Pho 76

Vietnamese Tofu Salad 77

Vietnamese Shrimp Soup 78

Vietnamese Rice-Noodle Salad 79

Vietnamese Lettuce Beef 80

Vietnamese Beef Pho 81

Vietnamese Chicken Wings 82

Vietnamese Chutney 83

Vietnamese Chicken & Curry Soup 84

Lemon Grass Chicken 85

La Sa Ga: A Vietnamese Pasta Soup 86

Vietnamese Coffee 87

Southeast Asian Rice Noodle Pesto 88

Vietnamese Vegetarian Curry Soup 89

Bo Nuong Xa: Mint and Basil Beef 90

Vietnamese Bean and Beef Stir Fry 91

Vietnamese Chicken Pho 92

Vietnamese Bamboo Tofu 93

Vietnamese Vermicelli 94

Southeast Asian Chicken Breast 95

Vietnamese Spring Rolls II 96

Vietnamese Sandwiches 97

Vietnamese Chicken and Rice Soup 98

Taiwanese Corn Soup: Creamy 99

Bo Luc Lac: Garlic Sirloin w/ Vinaigrette 100

Taiwanese Corn Soup II 101

Easy Egg and Pea Soup 102

Classical Egg Drop Soup 103

Hot and Spicy Soup 104

Korean BBQ Short Ribs (Galbi)

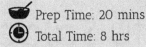
Prep Time: 20 mins
Total Time: 8 hrs

Servings per Recipe: 5
Calories   710 kcal
Fat   55.5 g
Carbohydrates   23.2g
Protein   28.8 g
Cholesterol   112 mg
Sodium   2231 mg

Ingredients

- 3/4 C. soy sauce
- 3/4 C. water
- 3 tbsps white vinegar
- 1/4 C. dark brown sugar
- 2 tbsps white sugar
- 1 tbsp black pepper
- 2 tbsps sesame oil
- 1/4 C. minced garlic
- 1/2 large onion, minced
- 3 lbs Korean-style short ribs

Directions

1. Get a bowl, combine: vinegar, water, soy sauce, onion, brown sugar, garlic, regular sugar, sesame oil, and regular pepper.
2. Add your ribs to this mix and cover the bowl with some plastic.
3. Place the contents in the fridge overnight.
4. Now grill the ribs for 6 mins per side on an oiled grate.
5. Enjoy.

SPICY
Tofu Salad

🍳 Prep Time: 10 mins
🕐 Total Time: 10 mins

Servings per Recipe: 1 bowl
Calories   198 kcal
Carbohydrates   23.7 g
Cholesterol   0 mg
Fat   7.2 g
Fiber   1.9 g
Protein   10.4 g
Sodium   472 mg

Ingredients

3 green onions, chopped
2 tbsps. soy sauce
2 tbsps. toasted sesame seeds
1 half tsps. Korean chili pepper powder, or to taste
1 tsp. white sugar
half tsp. toasted Asian sesame oil
1 half cups steamed Japanese rice
half head of romaine lettuce (heart only), torn into bite-size pieces
half cucumber - peeled, seeded, and chopped
1 (1 2 ounce) package tofu, sliced

Directions

1. Combine green onions, sesame seeds, Korean red pepper powder, soy sauce, sugar, and sesame oil in a regular sized bowl thoroughly
2. Now put the rice in bowl and add a mixture of lettuce and cucumber before putting tofu over it.
3. Now pour some sesame mixture over the tofu according to your tastes.

Korean Kimchee Squats

Prep Time: 25 mins
Total Time: 1 day 5 hrs

Servings per Recipe: 8
Calories	36 kcal
Carbohydrates	6.8 g
Cholesterol	0 mg
Fat	0.5 g
Fiber	1.9 g
Protein	2.6 g
Sodium	1796 mg

Ingredients

- 2 lbs. chopped Chinese cabbage
- 1 tbsp. salt
- 2 tbsps. chopped green onion
- 1 clove garlic, crushed
- 1 tbsp. chili powder
- 2 tsps. minced fresh ginger root
- half cup light soy sauce
- half cup white wine vinegar
- 2 tsps. white sugar
- 1 dash sesame oil

Directions

1. Let cabbage sit for 4 hours after adding some salt and massage it with your hands until you find that it is soft.
2. Now drain all the liquid and add green onion, soy sauce, sugar, ginger, garlic and chili powder into this cabbage.
3. Refrigerate for about 24 hours in a jar before serving.

KOREAN
Carrot Salad

🥣 Prep Time: 30 mins
⏲ Total Time: 30 mins

Servings per Recipe: 6
Calories   119 kcal
Carbohydrates   8.9 g
Cholesterol   0 mg
Fat   9.3 g
Fiber   2 g
Protein   0.8 g
Sodium   767 mg

Ingredients

1 lb. carrots, peeled and julienned (preferably with a mandolin)
three cloves garlic, minced
1/4 cup vinegar
1 tbsp. white sugar
2 half tsps. salt
1/three cup vegetable oil
half onion, minced
1 tsp. ground coriander
half tsp. cayenne pepper

Directions

1. Add garlic over carrots in a bowl and separately mix vinegar, sugar, and salt thoroughly.
2. Cook onions in hot oil for about 5 minutes and add coriander and cayenne pepper before adding everything to the carrot mixture.
3. Also add vinegar dressing over the mixture and refrigerate in a sealed dish for about 24 hours while tossing it several times.

Spicy Red Pepper Cucumbers

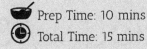
Prep Time: 10 mins
Total Time: 15 mins

Servings per Recipe: 2
Calories	1092 kcal
Carbohydrates	57.5 g
Cholesterol	155 mg
Fat	78.6 g
Fiber	1.8 g
Protein	39.1 g
Sodium	2501 mg

Ingredients

- 1 tsp. vegetable oil
- 2 tbsps. sesame seeds
- 2 tbsps. kochujang (Korean hot sauce)
- 1/4 cup white vinegar
- 1 tbsp. sesame oil
- 1 green onion, chopped
- 1 cucumber, halved, seeded and thinly sliced

Directions

1. Place sesame seeds in a large bowl after cooking in hot vegetable oil for about three minutes and add kochujang, green onion and sesame oil into the sesame seeds.
2. Now add cucumber and mix well.
3. Serve.

KOREAN Salad w/ Sesame Dressing

Prep Time: 10 mins
Total Time: 10 mins

Servings per Recipe: 5
Calories   80 kcal
Carbohydrates   6.1 g
Cholesterol   0 mg
Fat   5.9 g
Fiber   1.6 g
Protein   2 g
Sodium   740 mg

Ingredients

1 head red leaf lettuce
4 green onions (white part only)
1/4 cup soy sauce
5 tbsps. water
2 tsps. white sugar
1/4 cup distilled white vinegar
2 tbsps. sesame oil
1 tbsp. red pepper flakes

Directions

1. Place lettuce leaves into a bowl after washing and cutting.
2. Now add the sliced white portion of your sliced green onions into the bowl containing the lettuce leaves.
3. In a separate bowl mix soy sauce, white sugar, vinegar, sesame oil, water, and red pepper flakes and pour this mixture over the bowl containing lettuce leaves and green onions.
4. Serve.

Korean Cucumber Salad

Prep Time: 10 mins
Total Time: 40 mins

Servings per Recipe: 10
Calories	117 kcal
Carbohydrates	15.8 g
Cholesterol	0 mg
Fat	6.1 g
Fiber	1.7 g
Protein	2.1 g
Sodium	1332 mg

Ingredients

- three lbs. seedless cucumber, sliced paper-thin
- 1 half tbsps. sea salt
- half cup rice vinegar
- 1 tbsp. rice wine
- 2 tbsps. sesame oil
- 2 tbsps. honey
- 2 tbsps. freshly squeezed lemon juice
- 1 green onion, sliced
- 1 tbsp. toasted sesame seeds
- 2 walnut halves, finely chopped(optional)
- 1 clove garlic, minced
- 1 half tsps. Korean red pepper powder
- freshly ground black pepper to taste

Directions

1. Drain liquid from cucumbers after putting some sea salt by letting it stand for about 15 minutes and wrapping it in a paper towel to get more water out of it.
2. Now combine rice vinegar, rice wine, honey, green onion, sesame seeds, lemon juice, walnuts, garlic, sesame oil, Korean red pepper powder and ground black pepper in a medium sized bowl.
3. In this mixture, add cucumbers and refrigerate for at least 30 minutes after wrapping with plastic paper.

KIMCHEE JUN
Kimchee Pancakes

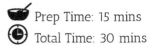
Prep Time: 15 mins
Total Time: 30 mins

Servings per Recipe: 8
Calories	199 kcal
Carbohydrates	26.5 g
Cholesterol	93 mg
Fat	7.1 g
Fiber	1.6 g
Protein	7.4 g
Sodium	513 mg

Ingredients

1 cup kimchi, drained and chopped
half cup reserved juice from kimchi
1 cup all-purpose flour
2 eggs
1 green onion, chopped
1 tbsp. vegetable oil
salt to taste
1 tbsp. rice vinegar
1 tbsp. soy sauce
half tsp. sesame oil

half tsp. Korean chili pepper flakes (optional)
half tsp. toasted sesame seeds (optional)

Directions

1. Combine kimchi, flour, eggs, kimchi juice and green onion in a medium sized bowl.
2. Cook pancakes made from ¼ cup of batter in hot vegetable oil for about 5 minutes each side.
3. Now combine rice vinegar, sesame oil, chili pepper flakes, soy sauce and toasted sesame seeds in a bowl and serve this with pancakes.

Jap Chae
Glass Noodles

🥣 Prep Time: 15 mins
🕐 Total Time: 20 mins

Servings per Recipe: 4
Calories	363 kcal
Carbohydrates	65.2 g
Cholesterol	0 mg
Fat	10.7 g
Fiber	0.6 g
Protein	1.9 g
Sodium	1073 mg

Ingredients

- 1 pkg. (8 serving size) sweet potato vermicelli
- half cup reduced-sodium soy sauce
- 1/4 cup brown sugar
- half cup boiling water
- three tbsps. vegetable oil
- 1 tsp. toasted sesame seeds

Directions

1. Cover the vermicelli with hot water after cutting it into small pieces for 10 minutes and add a mixture of soy sauce, boiling water, and brown sugar into it.
2. Cook this mixture in hot oil for about 5 minutes and just before serving, add noodles over it.

KONGNAMOOL
Korean Soybean Sprouts

Prep Time: 10 mins
Total Time: 10 mins

Servings per Recipe: 4
Calories   376 kcal
Carbohydrates   21.4 g
Cholesterol   69 mg
Fat   21.9 g
Fiber   0.8 g
Protein   20.6 g
Sodium   1249 mg

Ingredients
1 lb. soybean sprouts
2 tbsps. soy sauce
1/4 cup sesame oil
2 tbsps. Korean chili powder
1 half tsps. garlic, minced
2 tsps. sesame seeds
1/4 cup chopped green onion
2 tsps. rice wine vinegar, or to taste

Directions
1. Cook bean sprouts in salty boiling water for about 15 seconds and drain the water.
2. Put sprouts in ice cold water for about three minutes to stop the cooking process and when these bean sprouts are cold, set them aside.
3. Now combine soy sauce, sesame seeds, sesame oil and chili powder in a medium sized bowl and add bean sprouts to it.
4. Now add some green onion and rice wine vinegar before refrigerating for some time.
5. Serve

Bulgogi
Korean Chicken Stir Fry

Prep Time: 15 mins
Total Time: 30 mins

Servings per Recipe: 4
Calories   269 kcal
Fat   11.6 g
Carbohydrates   13.2 g
Protein   27.5 g
Cholesterol   69 mg
Sodium   1230 mg

Ingredients

- 1/4 C. diced onion
- 5 tbsps soy sauce
- 2 1/2 tbsps brown sugar
- 2 tbsps minced garlic
- 2 tbsps sesame oil
- 1 tbsp sesame seeds
- 1/2 tsp cayenne
- salt and ground black pepper to taste
- 1 lb skinless, boneless chicken breasts, cut into thin strips

Directions

1. Get a bowl, combine: black pepper, onions, salt, brown sugar, soy sauce, cayenne, garlic, sesame seeds, and sesame oils.
2. Add in your chicken to the mix and stir the mix before pouring everything in a wok.
3. Stir fry the contents until your chicken is fully done for about 17 mins.
4. Enjoy.

RED
Pepper Potatoes

Prep Time: 15 mins
Total Time: 35 mins

Servings per Recipe: 4
Calories   198 kcal
Carbohydrates   32.3 g
Cholesterol   0 mg
Fat   6.2 g
Fiber   5 g
Protein   4.6
Sodium   352 mg

Ingredients

1 half tbsps. soy sauce
1 pinch cayenne pepper, or to taste
1 half tbsps. vegetable oil
three potatoes, cut into bite sized pieces
4 green onions, chopped
1 large red bell pepper, chopped
2 tsps. sesame seeds

Directions

1. Mix cayenne pepper and soy sauce in a bowl and cook potatoes over hot vegetable oil for about 5 minutes or until golden.
2. Continue to cook for another minute after adding onion bell pepper and sesame seeds.
3. Add soy sauce mixture and cook for another 3 minutes.

Korean Fiddleheads

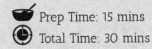
Prep Time: 15 mins
Total Time: 30 mins

Servings per Recipe: 3
Calories   376 kcal
Carbohydrates   21.4 g
Cholesterol   69 mg
Fat   21.9 g
Fiber   0.8 g
Protein   20.6 g
Sodium   1249 mg

Ingredients

three cups fresh fiddlehead ferns, ends trimmed
three tbsps. unfiltered extra-virgin olive oil
1 clove garlic, minced
half tsp. sea salt
half tsp. black pepper
1 tbsp. fresh lemon juice

Directions

1. Cook fiddlehead ferns in salty boiling water for about 10 minutes and drain the water.
2. Add pepper, and garlic in some hot olive oil along with the ferns for about 5 minutes and remove everything from the heat and add lemon juice before serving.

KOREAN
Crab Cakes

🥣 Prep Time: 15 mins
🕐 Total Time: 50 mins

Servings per Recipe: 4
Calories   254 kcal
Carbohydrates   9.6 g
Cholesterol   75 mg
Fat   17.4 g
Fiber   0.5 g
Protein   14.5 g
Sodium   620 mg

Ingredients

1/4 cup mayonnaise
2 tbsps. chopped fresh cilantro
1 tbsp. chopped fresh ginger
2 tsps. Asian fish sauce (nuoc mam or nam pla)
1 (6 ounce) can crabmeat - drained, flaked and cartilage removed
three ounces chopped shrimp
1 half cups fresh breadcrumbs, made from crustless French bread
salt and pepper to taste
1 half tbsps. peanut oil

Directions

1. Combine crab, shrimp, bread crumbs, fresh ginger, mayonnaise, fish sauce and cilantro together in a bowl before adding salt and pepper.
2. Take 1 fourth of a cup of this mixture and place in a bowl containing the remaining bread crumbs, and make a patty out of it.
3. Do the same for the rest of the crab mixture.
4. Now fry your patties in in hot oil over medium heat for about 5 minutes each side.
5. Serve

Korean Cashew Hummus

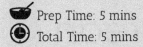
Prep Time: 5 mins
Total Time: 5 mins

Servings per Recipe: 3
Calories	270 kcal
Carbohydrates	28.6 g
Cholesterol	0 mg
Fat	16.5 g
Fiber	3 g
Protein	7.8 g
Sodium	367 mg

Ingredients
- 2 cups corn kernels, thawed if frozen
- 1 cup cashews
- 1 tsp. lemon juice, or more to taste
- 1/4 tsp. salt
- 1/4 tsp. onion powder
- 1/4 tsp. garlic powder

Directions
1. Place everything mentioned in a blender and blend it for about 1 minute.
2. Serve with rice.

BIBIMBAP
Korean Vegetable Hot Pot

🥣 Prep Time: 30 mins
⏱ Total Time: 50 mins

Servings per Recipe: 3
Calories   395 kcal
Fat   18.8 g
Carbohydrates   45g
Protein   13.6 g
Cholesterol   196 mg
Sodium   1086 mg

Ingredients

- 2 tbsps sesame oil
- 1 C. carrot matchsticks
- 1 C. zucchini matchsticks
- 1/2 (14 oz.) can bean sprouts, drained
- 6 oz. canned bamboo shoots, drained
- 1 (4.5 oz.) can sliced mushrooms, drained
- 1/8 tsp salt to taste
- 2 C. cooked and cooled rice
- 1/3 C. sliced green onions
- 2 tbsps soy sauce
- 1/4 tsp ground black pepper
- 1 tbsp butter
- 3 eggs
- 3 tsps sweet red chili sauce, or to taste

Directions

1. Stir fry your zucchini and carrots and in sesame oil for 7 mins then add in: mushrooms, bamboo, and sprouts.
2. Stir fry the mix for 7 more mins then add in some salt and remove the veggies from the pan.
3. Add in: black pepper, rice, soy sauce, and green onions. And get everything hot.
4. Now in another pan fry your eggs in butter. When the yolks are somewhat runny but the egg whites are cooked place the eggs to the side. This should take about 3 mins of frying.
5. Layer an egg on some rice.
6. Add the veggies on top of the egg and some red chili sauce over everything.
7. Enjoy.

Korean Vegetables

🍳 Prep Time: 20 mins
🕐 Total Time: 40 mins

Servings per Recipe: 6
Calories   106 kcal
Fat   4.9 g
Carbohydrates   14g
Protein   4 g
Cholesterol   0 mg
Sodium   1225 mg

Ingredients

5 medium zucchini, sliced
1 bunch green onions, sliced
1/4 C. white vinegar
1/2 C. soy sauce
1/4 C. water
2 tbsps sugar

2 tbsps sesame oil
ground black pepper to taste

Directions

1. Add the following to a big pot: sesame oil, zucchini, sugar, green onions, water, vinegar, and soy sauce.
2. Add in some black pepper as well.
3. Stir everything, then place a lid on the pot.
4. Let the contents cook with a low level of heat for about 22 mins until the veggies are soft.
5. Enjoy.

KOREAN
Whole Chicken

🥣 Prep Time: 10 mins
🕒 Total Time: 50 mins

Servings per Recipe: 4
Calories 794 kcal
Fat 54.7 g
Carbohydrates 6g
Protein 65.3 g
Cholesterol 1255 mg
Sodium 1338 mg

Ingredients

1 (3 lb) whole chicken, meat remove from the bones, slices in the 1/8" thick square pieces
1/4 C. soy sauce
2 tbsps sesame seeds
1/8 tsp salt
1/8 tsp ground black pepper
1 green onion, minced
1 clove garlic, minced
1 tsp peanut oil

1 tbsp white sugar
1 tsp monosodium glutamate (MSG)

Directions

1. Combine your cut chicken with some soy sauce in a bowl.
2. Now toast your sesame seeds in a pan.
3. Once they begin to pop place them in a bowl and top the seeds with salt.
4. Now mash the seeds with a big wooden spoon and add in: MSG, pepper, sugar, onions, oil, and garlic.
5. Now combine both bowls and let the chicken sit in the sesame mix for 35 mins.
6. Begin to stir fry your chicken in the same pan for 2 mins before placing a cover on the pot and cooking until the meat is fully done.
7. Enjoy.

Korean Pizzas

Prep Time: 10 mins
Total Time: 40 mins

Servings per Recipe: 8
Calories	233 kcal
Fat	7 g
Carbohydrates	30.1g
Protein	12.7 g
Cholesterol	63 mg
Sodium	663 mg

Ingredients

- 2 C. all-purpose flour
- 2 eggs
- 4 C. water
- 1/2 tsp salt
- 1 shallot, diced
- 1 green onion, diced
- 1/2 C. minced crabmeat
- 1/2 C. diced cooked pork
- 1/2 C. diced firm tofu
- 1 C. bean sprouts
- 1 C. frozen mixed vegetables, thawed
- 1/2 C. shredded cabbage
- 4 tsps canola oil
- 1/4 C. soy sauce
- 2 tbsps rice vinegar
- 1 tbsp sesame oil
- 1 chili pepper, diced (optional)

Directions

1. Get a bowl, combine: chili pepper, soy sauce, sesame oil, and vinegar. Place this mix to the side.
2. Get a 2nd bowl, combine: salt, flour, water, and eggs. Now add the: cabbage, crabmeat, mixed veggies, pork, sprouts, and tofu.
3. Now it is important that you get your oil very in a skillet then add in enough of the batter to coat the bottom of the pan.
4. Let this fry for 9 mins then flip it and cook for 4 more mins.
5. Continue with all of the remaining mix.
6. Finally top your dish with some of the sauce.
7. Enjoy.

SOON DU BU JIGAE
Tofu Stew

Prep Time: 5 mins
Total Time: 20 mins

Servings per Recipe: 2
Calories 242 kcal
Fat 16.5 g
Carbohydrates 7g
Protein 20 g
Cholesterol 99 mg
Sodium 415 mg

Ingredients

1 tsp vegetable oil
1 tsp Korean chile powder
2 tbsps ground beef (optional)
1 tbsp Korean soy bean paste (doenjang)
1 C. water
salt and pepper to taste
1 (12 oz.) package Korean soon tofu or soft tofu, drained and sliced
1 egg

1 tsp sesame seeds
1 green onion, diced

Directions

1. Stir fry your beef and chili powder in veggie oil until the beef is fully done then add the bean paste and stir.
2. Now add in the water and get everything boiling before adding in some pepper and salt.
3. Once the mix is boiling add in your tofu and cook the contents for 4 mins.
4. Shut the heat and crack your egg into the soup.
5. Stir everything and let the egg poach before adding a garnishing of green onions and sesame seeds.
6. Enjoy.

Chicken Stew Korean

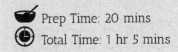

Prep Time: 20 mins
Total Time: 1 hr 5 mins

Servings per Recipe: 4
Calories   896 kcal
Fat   69.1 g
Carbohydrates   136.1g
Protein   33.4 g
Cholesterol   121 mg
Sodium   1111 mg

Ingredients

- 1 1/2 C. water
- 1/4 C. soy sauce
- 2 tbsps rice wine
- 2 tbsps Korean red chili pepper paste (gochujang)
- 2 tbsps Korean red chili pepper flakes (gochugaru)
- 1 tbsp honey
- 1 tbsp white sugar
- 1 pinch ground black pepper
- 3 lbs bone-in chicken pieces, trimmed of fat and cut into small pieces
- 10 oz. potatoes, cut into large chunks
- 2 carrots, cut into large chunks
- 1/2 large onion, cut into large chunks
- 4 large garlic cloves, or more to taste
- 2 slices fresh ginger, or more to taste
- 2 scallions, cut into 2-inch lengths
- 1 tbsp sesame oil
- 1 tsp sesame seeds

Directions

1. Get the following boiling in a big pot: chicken, water, black pepper, soy sauce, sugar, wine, honey, pepper paste, and pepper flakes.
2. Once everything is boiling set the heat to low and place a lid on the pot.
3. Let the contents cook for 17 mins.
4. Add in: ginger, potatoes, garlic, carrots, and onions and cook the mix for 17 more mins.
5. Take off the lid and continue cooking for 12 more mins.
6. Now add in some sesame seeds, scallions, and sesame oil.
7. Enjoy.

TUNA AND RICE (Chompchae Deopbap)

Prep Time: 10 mins
Total Time: 50 mins

Servings per Recipe: 2
Calories   562 kcal
Fat   9 g
Carbohydrates   87.5g
Protein   31.8 g
Cholesterol   25 mg
Sodium   1507 mg

Ingredients

- 1 C. uncooked white rice
- 2 C. water
- 1 tbsp olive oil
- 3 cloves garlic, minced
- 1 (1/2 inch) piece fresh ginger, minced
- 1/2 onion, coarsely diced
- 1 C. kim chee
- 1/2 C. sliced cucumber
- 1/4 C. sliced carrots
- 2 tbsps soy sauce
- 2 tbsps rice vinegar
- salt and pepper to taste
- 1 tbsp Korean chili powder, or to taste
- 1 tbsp water, or as needed
- 1 (6 oz.) can tuna, drained

Directions

1. Get your rice boiling with 2 C. of water, once it is boiling place a lid on the pot, set the heat to low, and let it cook for 23 mins.
2. Stir fry your onions, ginger, and garlic in olive oil for 7 mins then add in: vinegar, carrots, soy sauce, pepper, salt, chili powder, cucumbers, and kimchee.
3. Cook and add in your tuna, while stirring until everything is hot.
4. Layer the rice with a topping of tuna mix on each plate.
5. Enjoy.

Kalbi Jim
Korean Short Ribs II

🥣 Prep Time: 20 mins
🕐 Total Time: 1 hr 20 mins

Servings per Recipe: 6
Calories   647 kcal
Fat   54.9 g
Carbohydrates   14.1g
Protein   23.3 g
Cholesterol   115 mg
Sodium   805 mg

Ingredients

2 lbs beef short ribs, trimmed
1 green onion, diced
2 carrots, peeled and diced
4 cloves garlic, minced
1 (1 inch) piece fresh ginger root, diced
1/2 C. reduced-sodium soy sauce
1/4 C. brown sugar
2 C. water to cover

Directions

1. Cut some incisions into your beef then add them into a pan with: brown sugar, green onions, soy sauce, carrots, ginger, and garlic.
2. Add in some water to cover the contents and get everything boiling.
3. Once it is all boiling set the heat to low and let the contents cook for 60 mins.
4. Remove any excess oils then plate the contents.
5. Enjoy.

KOREAN
Burritos

🥣 Prep Time: 15 mins
🕐 Total Time: 30 mins

Servings per Recipe: 4
Calories 597 kcal
Fat 29.1 g
Carbohydrates 45.6g
Protein 38.5 g
Cholesterol 97 mg
Sodium 1635 mg

Ingredients

Meat:
6 cloves garlic, minced
2 tbsps Korean chili paste (gochujang)
1 tbsp soy sauce
2 tsps white sugar
1 tsp sesame oil
2 (10 oz.) cans chicken chunks, drained
Everything Else:
4 (10 inch) flour tortillas
2 tbsps vegetable oil

2 tsps butter, softened (optional)
1 C. fresh cilantro leaves
1/2 C. diced kimchi, squeezed dry (optional)
2 tbsps shredded sharp Cheddar cheese
1 tbsp salsa

Directions

1. Set your oven to 350 degrees before doing anything else.
2. Get a bowl, combine: sesame oil, garlic, sugar, soy sauce, and chili paste. Then add the chicken and stir everything.
3. Cover your tortillas with some foil and cook them for 12 mins in the oven.
4. At the same time begin to stir fry your chicken in veggie oil with the marinade.
5. Cook the chicken for about 12 mins as well.
6. Coat each tortilla with half a tsp of butter then add an equal amount of chicken to each.
7. Add the following to each tortilla before folding: salsa, cilantro, cheddar, and kimchi.
8. Shape everything into tacos and serve.
9. Enjoy.

Korean Curry

🥣 Prep Time: 20 mins
⏲ Total Time: 1 hr 20 mins

Servings per Recipe: 6
Calories   303 kcal
Fat   13.6 g
Carbohydrates   27.9 g
Protein   17.6 g
Cholesterol   36 mg
Sodium   60 mg

Ingredients

- 1/4 C. olive oil, divided
- 1 1/2 lbs boneless chicken breast, cut into cubes
- 1 large yellow onion, cut into cubes
- 2 large russet potatoes, peeled and cut into cubes
- 3 large carrots, peeled and cut into cubes
- 4 C. water
- 1 tbsp Korean-style curry powder (such as Assi(R) mild curry powder), or more to taste

Directions

1. Stir fry your chicken in 2 tbsps of olive oil for about 13 mins or until fully done.
2. Then in another pot stir fry your carrots, potatoes, and onions in more olive oil for 8 mins.
3. Add the chicken to the veggies and add some water.
4. Place a lid on the pot and let the contents gently boil for 22 mins.
5. Shut the heat and add in your curry and stir everything until the spice is completely mixed in.
6. Now cook everything for 25 more mins until the sauce is thick.
7. Enjoy.

YAKI MANDU
Korean Egg Rolls

Prep Time: 30 mins
Total Time: 45 mins

Servings per Recipe: 25
Calories	125 kcal
Fat	5.8 g
Carbohydrates	12.1g
Protein	5.7 g
Cholesterol	28 mg
Sodium	246 mg

Ingredients

1 lb ground beef
1 1/2 C. vegetable oil for frying
1/2 C. finely diced green onions
1/2 C. finely diced cabbage
1/2 C. finely diced carrot
1/2 C. minced garlic
4 tsps sesame oil, divided
1 tbsp toasted sesame seeds
1/2 tsp monosodium glutamate (such as Ac'cent(R))
salt and ground black pepper to taste
2 eggs
1 (16 oz.) package wonton wrappers
3 tbsps soy sauce
2 tsps rice wine vinegar
1 tsp toasted sesame seeds, or more to taste

Directions

1. Stir fry your beef for 8 mins.
2. At the same time in another pot for 12 mins cook: ground beef, green onions, pepper, cabbage, salt, carrots, MSG, garlic, 1 tbsp of sesame oil and seeds. Then remove everything from the pan.
3. Coat a wonton wrapper with some whisked egg and then add 1 tsp of beef mix into it.
4. Then fold everything into a triangle and crimp the edges.
5. Do this for all your ingredients.
6. Then for 3 mins per side fry the wontons then place layer them on some paper towels.
7. Get a bowl, combine: 1 tsp sesame seeds, soy sauce, 1 tsp sesame oil, and vinegar.
8. Use this as topping for your wontons.
9. Enjoy.

Korean Egg Rolls II

Prep Time: 45 mins
Total Time: 1 hr

Servings per Recipe: 6
Calories 534 kcal
Fat 28.4 g
Carbohydrates 56.9 g
Protein 14.6 g
Cholesterol 67 mg
Sodium 1177 mg

Ingredients

- 1/2 (8 oz.) package dry thin Asian rice noodles (rice vermicelli)
- 1/2 medium head cabbage, cored and shredded
- 1 (12 oz.) package firm tofu
- 2 small zucchini, shredded
- 4 green onions, finely diced
- 4 cloves garlic, finely diced
- 1 tbsp ground black pepper
- 2 tbsps Asian (toasted) sesame oil
- 2 eggs, slightly beaten
- 2 tsps salt
- 1 (12 oz.) package round wonton wrappers
- 1/2 C. vegetable oil for frying

Directions

1. Boil your noodles in water for 6 mins. Then remove all the liquids and run them under cold water.
2. Now dice the noodles and place everything to the side.
3. Squeeze your cabbage to drain any liquids and place them in a bowl with: noodles, tofu, salt, zucchini, eggs, sesame oil, green onions, black pepper, and garlic.
4. Mix everything with your hands and try to break up your tofu pieces.
5. Add 2 tsp of mix into your wonton wrappers and coat the edge with some water before shaping the wrapper into a triangle and crimping the edges.
6. Continue for all your ingredients then fry the wontons in veggie oil for 4 mins per side.
7. Enjoy.

HOW TO MAKE
Kimchee

🥣 Prep Time: 30 mins
🕐 Total Time: 3 days 3 hrs

Servings per Recipe: 30
Calories 6 kcal
Fat < 0 g
Carbohydrates < 1.5g
Protein < 0.3 g
Cholesterol < 0 mg
Sodium 932 mg

Ingredients

1 head Napa cabbage, cubed
1/4 C. salt, divided
6 cloves garlic
1 (1 inch) piece fresh ginger root, peeled and diced
1 small white onion, peeled and diced
2 tbsps water
3 green onions, minced
cayenne pepper to taste
1 ripe persimmon, diced
1 small radish, shredded
1 cucumber, diced (optional)

Directions

1. Get a bowl and combine your cabbage and salt.
2. Let it sit for 60 mins then add in more salt and let it stand for 60 more mins.
3. Now remove all the liquids and wash the leaves off.
4. Now blend the following until paste-like: onions, ginger, and garlic.
5. Add this to the cabbage along with: cucumbers, green onions, persimmon, cayenne, and radishes.
6. Place a covering on the bowl and let it sit in the fridge for at least 2 days.
7. Enjoy.

Chap Chee Noodles

Prep Time: 35 mins
Total Time: 1 hr

Servings per Recipe: 4
Calories	264 kcal
Fat	12.5 g
Carbohydrates	27.9 g
Protein	10.6 g
Cholesterol	23 mg
Sodium	1025 mg

Ingredients
- 1 tbsp soy sauce
- 1 tbsp sesame oil
- 2 green onions, finely diced
- 1 clove garlic, minced
- 1 tsp sesame seeds
- 1 tsp sugar
- 1/4 tsp black pepper
- 1/3 lb beef top sirloin, thinly sliced
- 2 tbsps vegetable oil
- 1/2 C. thinly sliced carrots
- 1/2 C. sliced bamboo shoots, drained
- 1/4 lb napa cabbage, sliced
- 2 C. diced fresh spinach
- 3 oz. cellophane noodles, soaked in warm water
- 2 tbsps soy sauce
- 1 tbsp sugar
- 1/2 tsp salt
- 1/4 tsp black pepper

Directions
1. Get a bowl, combine: a quarter of a C. of pepper, 1 tbsp of soy sauce, 1 tsp of sugar, sesame oil, sesame seeds, garlic, and green onions. Add in the beef and let the content sit for 17 mins.
2. Now stir fry the beef in oil until fill done then add in: spinach, carrots, cabbage, and bamboo. Cook for 2 more mins before add in: quarter tsp of pepper, half a tsp salt, 1 tbsps sugar, 2 tbsps of soy sauce, and noodles.
3. Set the heat to low and heat all the contents up.
4. Enjoy.

KOREAN
Sushi

🥣 Prep Time: 40 mins
🕐 Total Time: 1 hr

Servings per Recipe: 4
Calories   354 kcal
Fat   15.2 g
Carbohydrates   41.2g
Protein   11.9 g
Cholesterol   113 mg
Sodium   510 mg

Ingredients

1 C. uncooked glutinous white rice (sushi rice)
1 1/2 C. water
1 tbsp sesame oil
salt, to taste
2 eggs, beaten
4 sheets sushi nori (dry seaweed)
1 cucumber, cut into thin strips
1 carrot, cut into thin strips
4 slices American processed cheese, cut into thin strips
4 slices cooked ham, cut into thin strips, optional
2 tsps sesame oil

Directions

1. Get your water and rice boiling.
2. Once it is boiling, place a lid on the pot, and set the heat to low.
3. Let the rice cook for 15 mins.
4. Now pour the rice into a casserole dish to lose its heat.
5. At same time as the rice is cooking fry your eggs without stirring.
6. Place your nori sheet on a counter top and layer each with an equal amount of rice.
7. Now layer: ham, egg, cucumbers, cheese, and carrots.
8. Roll up the sheet with a bamboo mat and top each with half a tsp of sesame oil.
9. Dice up the roll into 6 pieces of sushi.
10. Enjoy.

Classical Pad Thai Noodles I

Prep Time: 35 mins
Total Time: 2 hrs

Servings per Recipe: 4
Calories   397 kcal
Carbohydrates   39.5 g
Cholesterol   41 mg
Fat   23.3 g
Fiber   5 g
Protein   13.2 g
Sodium   1234 mg

Ingredients

- 2/3 cup dried rice vermicelli
- 1/4 cup peanut oil
- 2/3 cup thinly sliced firm tofu
- 1 large egg, beaten
- 4 cloves garlic, finely chopped
- 1/4 cup vegetable broth
- 2 tbsps fresh lime juice
- 2 tbsps soy sauce
- 1 tbsp white sugar
- 1 tsp salt
- 1/2 tsp dried red chili flakes
- 3 tbsps chopped peanuts
- 1 pound bean sprouts, divided
- 3 green onions, whites cut thinly across and greens sliced into thin lengths - divided
- 3 tbsps chopped peanuts
- 2 limes, cut into wedges for garnish

Directions

1. Put rice vermicelli noodles in hot water for about 30 minutes before draining the water.
2. Cook tofu in hot oil until golden brown before draining it with paper tower.
3. Reserve 1 tbsp of oil for later use and cook egg in the remaining hot oil until done, and set them aside for later use.
4. Now cook noodles and garlic in the hot reserved oil, while coating them well with this oil along the way.
5. In this pan containing noodles; add tofu, salt, chili flakes, egg and 3 tbsps peanuts, and mix all this very thoroughly.
6. Also add bean sprouts and green onion into it, while reserving some for the garnishing purposes.
7. Cook all this for two minutes before transferring to a serving platter.
8. Garnish this with peanuts and the reserved vegetables before placing some lime wedges around the platter to make this dish more attractive.
9. Serve.

GALBI
Korean Short Ribs III

Prep Time: 1 hr
Total Time: 10 hrs

Servings per Recipe: 6
Calories   1092 kcal
Fat   78.6 g
Carbohydrates   157.5g
Protein   39.1 g
Cholesterol   155 mg
Sodium   2501 mg

Ingredients

5 lbs beef short ribs, cut flanken style
5 cloves garlic
1 onion, coarsely diced
1 Asian pear, cored and cubed
1 C. soy sauce (such as Kikkoman(R))
1 C. brown sugar
1/4 C. honey
1/4 C. sesame oil
black pepper to taste

Directions

1. Submerge your ribs in water for 60 mins then then drain them.
2. Puree the following in a blender: pear, onions, and garlic. Add this to a bowl with: black pepper, soy sauce, sesame oil, brown sugar, and honey. Place your ribs in the mix and let it sit in the fridge for 8 hrs with a covering of plastic.
3. Now grill your beef on an oiled grate for 7 mins per side.
4. Enjoy.

Easy Hummus Thai Style

Prep Time: 15 mins
Total Time: 30 mins

Servings per Recipe: 12
Calories   142 kcal
Carbohydrates   13.8 g
Cholesterol   0 mg
Fat   9.4 g
Fiber   2.4 g
Protein   3.9 g
Sodium   315 mg

Ingredients

- 1/4 cup coconut oil
- 2 large cloves garlic, very thinly sliced
- 2 cups cooked garbanzo beans
- 1/4 cup fresh lime juice
- 1/4 cup peanut butter
- 1/4 cup coconut milk
- 1/4 cup sweet chili sauce
- 1/4 cup minced lemon grass
- 1/4 cup minced fresh Thai basil leaves
- 1 tbsp grated fresh ginger
- 2 tsps green curry paste
- 1 jalapeno pepper, minced
- 1/2 tsp salt
- 1 pinch cayenne pepper (optional)
- 1 pinch chili powder (optional)

Directions

1. Cook garlic in hot coconut oil for about one minute and transfer it to a bowl.
2. Put cooled garlic mixture, lime juice, coconut milk, chili sauce, lemon grass, basil, ginger, curry paste, garbanzo beans, jalapeno pepper, salt, peanut butter, cayenne pepper and chili in a blender and blend it until you find that it is smooth.
3. Serve.

FRESH
Thai Pesto

Prep Time: 10 mins
Total Time: 10 mins

Servings per Recipe: 12
Calories   84 kcal
Carbohydrates   3.4 g
Cholesterol   0 mg
Fat   7.4 g
Fiber   0.6 g
Protein   1.9 g
Sodium   197 mg

Ingredients
1 bunch cilantro
1/4 cup peanut butter
3 cloves garlic, minced
3 tbsps extra-virgin olive oil
2 tbsps minced fresh ginger
1 1/2 tbsps fish sauce
1 tbsp brown sugar
1/2 tsp cayenne pepper

Directions
1. Put all the ingredients that are mentioned above in a blender and blend it until you see that the required smoothness is achieved.

Curry Thai Chicken with Pineapple

Prep Time: 15 mins
Total Time: 50 mins

Servings per Recipe: 6
Calories	623 kcal
Carbohydrates	77.5 g
Cholesterol	20 mg
Fat	34.5 g
Fiber	3.5 g
Protein	20.3 g
Sodium	781 mg

Ingredients

- 2 cups uncooked jasmine rice
- 1 quart water
- 1/4 cup red curry paste
- 2 (13.5 ounce) cans coconut milk
- 2 skinless, boneless chicken breast halves - cut into thin strips
- 3 tbsps fish sauce
- 1/4 cup white sugar
- 1 1/2 cups sliced bamboo shoots, drained
- 1/2 red bell pepper, julienned
- 1/2 green bell pepper, julienned
- 1/2 small onion, chopped
- 1 cup pineapple chunks, drained

Directions

1. Bring the mixture of rice and water to boil before turning the heat down to low and cooking for 25 minutes.
2. Add coconut milk, bamboo shoots, chicken, sugar and fish sauce to the mixture of curry paste and 1 can coconut milk in a pan before bringing all this to boil and cooking for 15 minutes.
3. Into this mixture, add red bell pepper, onion and green bell pepper, and cook all this for ten more minutes or until you see that the peppers are tender.
4. Add pineapple after removing from heat and serve this on top of cooked rice.

CLASSICAL
Pad Thai Noodle II

🥣 Prep Time: 15 mins
⏱ Total Time: 25 mins

Servings per Recipe: 4
Calories   352 kcal
Carbohydrates   46.8 g
Cholesterol   46 mg
Fat   15 g
Fiber   3 g
Protein   9.2 g
Sodium   335 mg

Ingredients

1 (6.75 ounce) package thin rice noodles
2 tbsps vegetable oil
3 ounces fried tofu, sliced into thin strips
1 clove garlic, minced
1 egg
1 tbsp soy sauce
1 pinch white sugar
2 tbsps chopped peanuts
1 cup fresh bean sprouts
1 tbsp chopped fresh cilantro
1 lime, cut into wedges

Directions

1. In a heatproof bowl containing noodles, pour boiling water and let it stand as it is for about five minutes before draining the water and setting it aside for later use.
2. Fry garlic in hot oil until brown before adding noodles frying it for about one minute.
3. Now add egg into it and break it up when it starts to get solid, and mix it well into the noodles.
4. Now add soy sauce, tofu, cilantro, bean sprouts, sugar and peanuts into it and mix it well.
5. Remove from heat and add lime wedges just before you serve.

Brown Rice Vegetable Soup

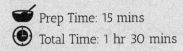

Prep Time: 15 mins
Total Time: 1 hr 30 mins

Servings per Recipe: 12
Calories	183 kcal
Carbohydrates	21.4 g
Cholesterol	< 1 mg
Fat	7.4 g
Fiber	3 g
Protein	4.4 g
Sodium	749 mg

Ingredients

- 1 cup uncooked brown rice
- 2 cups water
- 3 tbsps olive oil
- 1 sweet onion, chopped
- 4 cloves garlic, minced
- 1/4 cup chopped fresh ginger root
- 1 cup chopped carrots
- 4 cups chopped broccoli
- 1 red bell pepper, diced
- 1 (14 ounce) can light coconut milk
- 6 cups vegetable broth
- 1 cup white wine
- 3 tbsps fish sauce
- 2 tbsps soy sauce
- 3 Thai chili peppers
- 2 tbsps chopped fresh lemon grass
- 1 tbsp Thai pepper garlic sauce
- 1 tsp saffron
- 3/4 cup plain yogurt
- fresh cilantro, for garnish

Directions

1. Bring the mixture of rice and water to boil before turning the heat down to low and cooking for 45 minutes.
2. Cook ginger, carrots, garlic and onion in hot olive oil for about five minutes before you add broccoli, coconut milk, broth, wine, soy sauce, Thai chili peppers, red bell pepper, lemon grass, fish sauce, garlic sauce, and saffron into it and cook for another 25 minutes.
3. Now blend this soup in batches in a blender until you get the required smoothness.
4. Mix yoghurt and cooked rice very thoroughly with this soup.
5. Garnish with cilantro before you serve.

HOW TO MAKE
Peanut Sauce

Prep Time: 10 mins
Total Time: 10 mins

Servings per Recipe: 6
Calories	130 kcal
Carbohydrates	9.8 g
Cholesterol	3 mg
Fat	9.5 g
Fiber	0.6 g
Protein	2.7 g
Sodium	529 mg

Ingredients
- 1/4 cup creamy peanut butter
- 3 cloves garlic, minced
- 1/4 cup brown sugar
- 1/4 cup mayonnaise
- 1/4 cup soy sauce
- 2 tbsps fresh lemon juice

Directions
1. Whisk all the ingredients that are mentioned above in a medium sized bowl and refrigerate it for at least two hours before you serve it to anyone.

Thai Style Broccoli Mix

Prep Time: 10 mins
Total Time: 30 mins

Servings per Recipe: 4
Calories   315 kcal
Carbohydrates   8.2 g
Cholesterol   65 mg
Fat   18.9 g
Fiber   3.2 g
Protein   28.3 g
Sodium   275 mg

Ingredients

2 tbsps olive oil
2 large skinless, boneless chicken breast halves, cut into bite-size pieces
1 (12 ounce) package broccoli coleslaw mix
1 tsp sesame oil, or to taste
1/2 cup water
1/2 cup peanut sauce (such as House of Tsang®), or to taste
1 pinch salt to taste

Directions

1. Cook chicken in hot olive oil for about 5 minutes before you add water, broccoli and sesame oil.
2. Cook this on medium heat for about 15 minutes or until you see that the broccoli slaw is tender.
3. Do add some peanut sauce and salt according to your taste before serving.

THAI
Orange Chicken

🥣 Prep Time: 15 mins
🕐 Total Time: 40 mins

Servings per Recipe: 12
Calories   427 kcal
Carbohydrates   37.1 g
Cholesterol   32 mg
Fat   24.3 g
Fiber   3.5 g
Protein   18.4 g
Sodium   1360 mg

Ingredients

2 tbsps olive oil
3 carrots, cut into matchsticks
1/2 tsp minced fresh ginger root
1 clove garlic, minced
2 tbsps olive oil
2 skinless, boneless chicken breast halves, cut into small pieces
1/2 cup water
1/2 cup peanuts
1/3 cup orange juice

1/3 cup soy sauce
1/3 cup brown sugar
2 tbsps ketchup
1 tsp crushed red pepper flakes
2 tbsps cornstarch

Directions

1. Cook carrots, garlic and ginger in hot olive oil for about 5 minutes before transferring it to a bowl.
2. Cook chicken in hot olive oil for about 10 minutes before adding carrot mixture, water, brown sugar , orange juice, soy sauce, peanuts, ketchup, and red pepper flakes into this, and cooking for another 5 minutes.
3. Take out ¼ cup of sauce from the pan and add cornstarch into it.
4. Add this cornstarch mixture back to the chicken and cook until you see that the required thickness has been reached.

Thai BBQ Chicken

Prep Time: 15 mins
Total Time: 4 hrs 15 mins

Servings per Recipe: 4
Calories	564 kcal
Carbohydrates	52.4 g
Cholesterol	230 mg
Fat	19.3 g
Fiber	4.3 g
Protein	46.3 g
Sodium	375 mg

Ingredients
- 1 bunch fresh cilantro with roots
- 3 cloves garlic, peeled
- 3 small red hot chili peppers, seeded and chopped
- 1 tsp ground turmeric
- 1 tsp curry powder
- 1 tbsp white sugar
- 1 pinch salt
- 3 tbsps fish sauce
- 1 (3 pound) chicken, cut into pieces
- 1/4 cup coconut milk

Directions
1. At first you need to set a grill or grilling plate to medium heat and put some oil before starting anything else.
2. Put minced cilantro roots, salt, leaves, chili peppers, curry powder, turmeric, sugar, fish sauce, garlic in a blender and blend until you see that the required smoothness is achieved.
3. Combine this paste and chicken in large bowl, and refrigerate it for at least three hours for margination.
4. Cook this on the preheated grill for about 15 minutes each side or until tender, while brushing it regularly with coconut milk.
5. Serve.

NOTE: Adjust grilling times accordingly if using a grilling plate instead of a conventional grill.

THAI
Cucumber Soup

🥣 Prep Time: 15 mins
🕐 Total Time: 45 mins

Servings per Recipe: 4
Calories	67 kcal
Carbohydrates	6.8 g
Cholesterol	3 mg
Fat	4 g
Fiber	1.4 g
Protein	1.7 g
Sodium	702 mg

Ingredients
1 tbsp vegetable oil
3 cucumbers, peeled and diced
1/2 cup chopped green onion
2 1/2 cups chicken broth
1 1/2 tbsps lemon juice
1 tsp white sugar
salt and ground black pepper to taste

Directions
1. Cook cucumber in hot olive oil for about 5 minutes before adding green onions and cooking for another five minutes.
2. Add chicken broth, sugar and lemon juice into it before bringing all this to boil.
3. Turn down the heat to low and cook for another 20 minutes before adding salt and black pepper according to your taste.
4. Serve.

Thai Chicken Curry

Prep Time: 15 mins
Total Time: 55 mins

Servings per Recipe: 6
Calories 500 kcal
Carbohydrates 22.1 g
Cholesterol 58 mg
Fat 36.1 g
Fiber 3.6 g
Protein 25.8 g
Sodium 437 mg

Ingredients

- 1 tbsp olive oil
- 3 tbsps Thai yellow curry paste (such as Mae Ploy®)
- 1 pound cooked skinless, boneless chicken breast, cut into bite-size pieces
- 2 (14 ounce) cans coconut milk
- 1 cup chicken stock
- 1 yellow onion, chopped
- 3 small red potatoes, cut into cubes, or as needed
- 3 red Thai chili peppers, chopped with seeds, or more to taste
- 1 tsp fish sauce

Directions

1. Mix curry paste in hot oil before adding chicken and coating it well.
2. Add 1 can coconut milk and cook it for five minutes before adding the rest of the coconut milk, onion, potatoes, chicken stock and chili peppers into it and bringing all this to boil.
3. Turn the heat down to low and cook for 25 minutes or until the potatoes are tender.
4. Add fish sauce into before serving.
5. Enjoy..

CHARONG'S
Ginger Soup

🥣 Prep Time: 15 mins
🕐 Total Time: 25 mins

Servings per Recipe: 4
Calories	415 kcal
Carbohydrates	7.3 g
Cholesterol	29 mg
Fat	39 g
Fiber	2.1 g
Protein	14.4 g
Sodium	598 mg

Ingredients

3 cups coconut milk
2 cups water
1/2 pound skinless, boneless chicken breast halves - cut into thin strips
3 tbsps minced fresh ginger root
2 tbsps fish sauce, or to taste
1/4 cup fresh lime juice
2 tbsps sliced green onions
1 tbsp chopped fresh cilantro

Directions

1. Bring the mixture of coconut milk and water to boil before adding chicken strips, and cooking it for three minutes on medium heat or until you see that the chicken is cooked through.
2. Now add ginger, green onions, lime juice, cilantro and fish sauce into it.
3. Mix it well and serve.

Thai Veggie Soup

Prep Time: 15 mins
Total Time: 55 mins

Servings per Recipe: 5
Calories	310 kcal
Carbohydrates	22.9 g
Cholesterol	55 mg
Fat	22.4 g
Fiber	5.7 g
Protein	8.5 g
Sodium	147 mg

Ingredients

- 1/4 cup butter
- 6 tomatoes, peeled and quartered
- 3 zucchini, cut into chunks
- 1 yellow onion, cut in half and quartered
- 1 red bell pepper, chopped
- 3 cloves garlic, roughly chopped
- 1/4 cup chopped fresh cilantro leaves
- 1 tbsp chopped fresh basil (preferably Thai basil)
- 1 tbsp lime juice
- 1 pinch salt
- 2 1/2 cups milk
- 3 tbsps coconut butter
- 1 tbsp curry powder
- 1/4 tsp ground turmeric
- 1/4 tsp ground ginger
- 1/8 tsp ground cumin
- 1 bay leaf
- 5 tbsps heavy whipping cream (optional)

Directions

1. Cook tomatoes, zucchini, onion, garlic, cilantro, red bell pepper, basil, lime juice, and salt in hot butter for about 25 minutes before transferring it to a blender and blending it until the required smoothness is achieved.
2. Cook milk, curry powder, turmeric, ginger, coconut butter, cumin, and bay leaf in the same pan for about 5 minutes or until you see that coconut butter has melted.
3. At the very end, add blended vegetables into it and cook for five more minutes.
4. Garnish with heavy cream before serving.

THAI
Chicken Curry II

🥣 Prep Time: 15 mins
🕐 Total Time: 35 mins

Servings per Recipe: 4
Calories   621 kcal
Carbohydrates   86.7 g
Cholesterol   91 mg
Fat   19.4 g
Fiber   2.1 g
Protein   35.2 g
Sodium   316 mg

Ingredients

1 tbsp canola oil
2 tbsps green curry paste
1 pound boneless skinless chicken breasts, cut into bite-size pieces
1 small onion, thinly sliced
1 red pepper, cut into thin strips, then cut crosswise in half
1 green pepper, cut into thin strips, then cut crosswise in half
4 ounces cream cheese, cubed
1/4 cup milk
1/8 tsp white pepper
2 cups hot cooked long-grain white rice

Directions

1. Combine curry paste and hot oil before adding chicken and onions.
2. Cook this for about 8 minutes before adding green and red peppers, and cooking for another five minutes.
3. Now add cream cheese, white pepper and milk, and cook until you see that the cheese has melted.
4. Serve this on top of rice.
5. Enjoy.

Classical Shrimp in Thailand

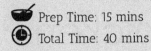 Prep Time: 15 mins
Total Time: 40 mins

Servings per Recipe: 4
Calories	289 kcal
Carbohydrates	8.2 g
Cholesterol	173 mg
Fat	20.1 g
Fiber	2.1 g
Protein	20.9 g
Sodium	502 mg

Ingredients

- 4 cloves garlic, peeled
- 1 (1 inch) piece fresh ginger root
- 1 fresh jalapeno pepper, seeded
- 1/2 tsp salt
- 1/2 tsp ground turmeric
- 2 tbsps vegetable oil
- 1 medium onion, diced
- 1 pound medium shrimp - peeled and deveined
- 2 tomatoes, seeded and diced
- 1 cup coconut milk
- 3 tbsps chopped fresh basil leaves

Directions

1. Blend the mixture of garlic, turmeric, ginger and jalapeno in a blender until the required smoothness is achieved.
2. Cook onion in hot oil for a few minutes before adding spice paste and cooking for another few minutes.
3. Cook shrimp for a few minutes in it before adding tomatoes and coconut milk, and cooking it for five minutes covered with lid.
4. Now cook for five more minutes without lid to get the sauce thick.
5. Also add some fresh basil at the last minute.
6. Serve.

THAI
Chicken Patties

🥣 Prep Time: 15 mins
🕐 Total Time: 35 mins

Servings per Recipe: 8
Calories   612 kcal
Carbohydrates   50.9 g
Cholesterol   80 mg
Fat   35.4 g
Fiber   2 g
Protein   36.5 g
Sodium   859 mg

Ingredients

1 cup mayonnaise
1/4 cup flaked coconut, finely chopped
1 tbsp chopped fresh mint
2 pounds ground chicken
2 1/2 cups panko bread crumbs
1/2 cup Thai peanut sauce
2 tbsps red curry paste
2 tbsps minced green onion
2 tbsps minced fresh parsley
2 tsps soy sauce

3 cloves garlic, minced
2 tsps lemon juice
2 tsps lime juice
1 tbsp hot pepper sauce
8 hamburger buns, split and toasted

Directions

1. At first you need to set a grill or grilling plate to medium heat and put some oil before starting anything else.
2. Refrigerate a mixture of mayonnaise, mint and coconut for one hour.
3. Combine ground chicken, Thai peanut sauce, curry paste, parsley, soy sauce, garlic, lemon juice, green onion, panko crumbs, lime juice, and hot pepper sauce in large sized bowl.
4. Cook this on the preheated grill for about 8 minutes each side or until tender.
5. Serve this with toasted bun.

NOTE: Adjust grilling times accordingly if using a grilling plate instead of a conventional grill.

Homemade Thai Pizzas

🥣 Prep Time: 15 mins
🕐 Total Time: 30 mins

Servings per Recipe: 8
Calories   396 kcal
Carbohydrates   33.3 g
Cholesterol   37 mg
Fat   20.2 g
Fiber   3.3 g
Protein   24.2 g
Sodium   545 mg

Ingredients

- 1 (12 inch) pre-baked pizza crust
- 1 (7 ounce) jar peanut sauce
- 1/4 cup peanut butter
- 8 ounces cooked skinless, boneless chicken breast halves, cut into strips
- 1 cup shredded Italian cheese blend
- 1 bunch green onions, chopped
- 1/2 cup fresh bean sprouts(optional)
- 1/2 cup shredded carrot(optional)
- 1 tbsp chopped roasted peanuts (optional)

Directions

1. Preheat your oven to 400 degrees F.
2. Spread a mixture of peanut sauce and peanut butter over the pizza crust and also put some strips of chicken, green onions and cheese.
3. Bake in the preheated oven for about 12 minutes or until the cheese has melted.
4. Garnish with carrot shreds, peanuts and sprouts.
5. Serve.

FRESH
Basil Chicken

Prep Time: 15 mins
Total Time: 20 mins

Servings per Recipe: 4
Calories   273 kcal
Carbohydrates   16.5 g
Cholesterol   69 mg
Fat   10.7 g
Fiber   2.4 g
Protein   29.4 g
Sodium   769 mg

Ingredients

2 tbsps peanut oil
1/4 cup minced garlic
1 pound ground chicken breast
12 Thai chilis, sliced into thin rings
2 tsps black soy sauce
2 tbsps fish sauce
1 cup fresh basil leaves

Directions

1. Cook garlic in hot peanut oil for about twenty seconds before adding ground chicken and cooking for another two minutes or until the chicken loses any pinkness.
2. Now add sliced chilies, fish sauce and soy sauce into it before cooking for 15 seconds to get the chilies tender.
3. At the very end, add basil and cook until you see that basil has wilted.
4. Serve.

Easy Coconut Soup II

Prep Time: 35 mins
Total Time: 1 hrs 5 mins

Servings per Recipe: 8
Calories   375 kcal
Fat   33.2 g
Carbohydrates   9.4g
Protein   13.7 g
Cholesterol   89 mg
Sodium   1059 mg

Ingredients

- 1 tbsp vegetable oil
- 2 tbsps grated fresh ginger
- 1 stalk lemon grass, minced
- 2 tsps red curry paste
- 4 C. chicken broth
- 3 tbsps fish sauce
- 1 tbsp light brown sugar
- 3 (13.5 oz.) cans coconut milk
- 1/2 lb fresh shiitake mushrooms, sliced
- 1 lb medium shrimp - peeled and deveined
- 2 tbsps fresh lime juice
- salt to taste
- 1/4 C. chopped fresh cilantro

Directions

1. Stir fry your curry paste, lemongrass, and ginger in oil for 2 mins then add in the broth while continuing to stir everything.
2. Add in the brown sugar and fish sauce and let the contents gently boil for 17 mins.
3. Now add the mushrooms and the coconut milk.
4. Continue cooking everything for 7 more min.
5. Then combine in the shrimp and let the fish cook for 7 mins until it is fully done.
6. Now add some cilantro, salt, and lime juice.
7. Enjoy.

SPICY
Pasta Thai

🥣 Prep Time: 15 mins
🕒 Total Time: 20 mins

Servings per Recipe: 8
Calories   564 kcal
Carbohydrates   52.4 g
Cholesterol   230 mg
Fat   19.3 g
Fiber   4.3 g
Protein   46.3 g
Sodium   375 mg

Ingredients
1 (12 ounce) package rice vermicelli
1 large tomato, diced
4 green onions, diced
2 pounds cooked shrimp, peeled and deveined
1 1/2 cups prepared Thai peanut sauce

Directions
1. Add rice vermicelli into boiling water and cook for about five minutes or until done.
2. Combine this rice with tomato, peanut sauce, green onions and shrimp very thoroughly in a medium sized bowl before refrigerating for at least eight hours.

Fried Chicken from Thailand

Prep Time: 15 mins
Total Time: 4 hrs 50 mins

Servings per Recipe: 4
Calories   1032 kcal
Fat   47.5 g
Carbohydrates   102.1g
Protein   76.1 g
Cholesterol   1292 mg
Sodium   1428 mg

Ingredients

- 1/2 C. honey mustard
- 1/2 C. sweet chili sauce
- 2 eggs, beaten
- sea salt to taste
- 12 chicken drumsticks
- 4 C. panko bread crumbs
- 4 C. vegetable oil for frying

Directions

1. Get a bowl, combine: sea salt, honey mustard, eggs, and chili sauce. Stir the mix until it is smooth and even then pour the mix into a plastic bag. Add your chicken to the bag and squeeze out all the air. Seal the bag then place everything in the fridge for 5 hrs.
2. Now set your oven to 350 degrees before doing anything else.
3. Get a dish layer your bread crumbs in it. Coat your pieces of chicken with the flour then begin to fry the chicken in hot veggie oil for 9 mins. Now place the meat on a cookie sheet and cook everything in the oven for 40 mins.
4. Enjoy.

SPICY
Lime Shrimp

🥣 Prep Time: 1 hr 5 mins
🕐 Total Time: 1 hr 25 mins

Servings per Recipe: 8
Calories 535 kcal
Fat 39.4 g
Carbohydrates 14.9 g
Protein 29.2 g
Cholesterol 173 mg
Sodium 648 mg

Ingredients

- 1/4 C. minced lemon grass (white part only)
- 1/4 C. minced fresh ginger root
- 2 tbsps minced garlic
- 1/4 tbsp chopped fresh cilantro
- 1 Thai or serrano chili pepper, minced
- 3/4 C. peanut or canola oil
- 2 lbs extra large shrimp (16 - 20), peeled and deveined, tail left on
- 1/4 C. lime juice
- 1/4 C. rice wine vinegar
- 1/2 C. mirin (Japanese sweet wine)
- 2 tbsps dark soy sauce
- 2 tbsps cold water
- 3 tbsps grated lime zest
- 1 tbsp minced fresh ginger root
- 2 tsps fish sauce
- 2 fresh Thai or Serrano chili, seeds removed
- 2 tsps minced garlic
- 1/2 C. smooth, unsalted peanut butter
- 1/4 C. peanut oil
- 2 tbsps chopped fresh mint
- 1 tbsp chopped fresh cilantro
- 1/4 C. unsalted roasted peanuts, chopped
- Kosher salt to taste

Directions

1. Get a bowl, combine: 3/4 C. of peanut oil, lemon grass, 1 minced chili, 1/4 C. of ginger, cilantro, and garlic.
2. Stir in the shrimp to the mix and place a covering of plastic over everything.
3. Let the bowl sit for 40 mins.
4. At the same time begin to pulse the following in a food processor: water, lime juice, soy sauce, mirin, and rice vinegar.
5. Get the mix smooth then add in: peanut butter, lime zest, garlic, 1 tbsp ginger, 2 chili peppers, and fish sauce.
6. Continue pulsing until everything is smooth again.
7. Now set the processor to a low speed and gradually add in the peanut oil in an even stream.

8. Once the mix is creamy enter everything into a bowl. Then add in: pepper, mint, salt, cilantro, and chopped peanuts.
9. Cook your pieces of fish on the grill for 4 mins each side. When eating the shrimp dip the pieces in the peanut sauce.
10. Enjoy.

HONEY CHILI
Peanut Noodles

🥣 Prep Time: 15 mins
🕒 Total Time: 25 mins

Servings per Recipe: 4
Calories   330 kcal
Fat   12 g
Carbohydrates   46.8g
Protein   10.7 g
Cholesterol   0 mg
Sodium   1188 mg

Ingredients
1/2 C. chicken broth
1 1/2 tbsps minced fresh ginger root
3 tbsps soy sauce
3 tbsps peanut butter
1 1/2 tbsps honey
2 tsps hot chili paste (optional)
3 cloves garlic, minced
8 oz. Udon noodles
1/4 C. chopped green onions
1/4 C. chopped peanuts

Directions
1. Boil your noodles in water for 9 mins then remove all the liquids.
2. At the same time begin to stir and heat the following in a pan: garlic, broth, chili paste, ginger, honey, soy sauce, and peanut butter.
3. Once the mix is hot and smooth add in your noodles when they are finished. Then stir everything to evenly distribute the sauce.
4. Now top the noodles with some peanuts and onions.
5. Enjoy.

Thai Sweet Short Grain

Prep Time: 10 mins
Total Time: 1 hrs 30 mins

Servings per Recipe: 4
Calories   817 kcal
Fat   26 g
Carbohydrates   144.3g
Protein   8.4 g
Cholesterol   0 mg
Sodium   458 mg

Ingredients

- 1 1/2 C. uncooked short-grain white rice
- 2 C. water
- 1 1/2 C. coconut milk
- 1 C. white sugar
- 1/2 tsp salt
- 1/2 C. coconut milk
- 1 tbsp white sugar
- 1/4 tsp salt
- 1 tbsp tapioca starch
- 3 mangos, peeled and sliced
- 1 tbsp toasted sesame seeds

Directions

1. Get your rice boiling in water, set the heat to low, place a lid on the pot, and let the rice cook for 17 mins.
2. At the same time get the following boiling: 1/2 tsp salt, 1.5 C. coconut milk, and 1 C. of sugar.
3. Stir the mix as it heats. Then once everything is boiling shut the heat.
4. Add the rice to the mix once it is done cooking, stir the mix, and let everything sit for 60 mins.
5. Get a separate pan and begin to get the following boiling: 1/4 tsp salt, 1/2 C. coconut milk, 1 tbsp sugar, and tapioca.
6. Once the mix has boiled for a few mins and is thick layer your rice on a plate.
7. Place some mango on top of the rice and top everything with the sauce.
8. Garnish the dish with the sesame seeds.
9. Enjoy.

THAI
Lunch Box
(Peanut, Jalapeno, and Cucumber Salad)

Prep Time: 15 mins
Total Time: 45 mins

Servings per Recipe: 4
Calories   238 kcal
Fat   9.4 g
Carbohydrates   37.1 g
Protein   5.8 g
Cholesterol   0 mg
Sodium   1751 mg

Ingredients
3 large cucumbers, peeled, halved lengthwise, seeded, and cut into 1/4-inch slices
1 tbsp salt
1/2 C. white sugar
1/2 C. rice wine vinegar
2 jalapeno peppers, seeded and chopped
1/4 C. chopped cilantro
1/2 C. chopped peanuts

Directions
1. Get a perforated bowl and in the sink combine your salt and cucumbers.
2. Let the mix sit for 40 mins then run the veggies under some fresh water.
3. Now dry everything with some paper towels.
4. Get a bowl, combine: vinegar and sugar.
5. Continue mixing everything until the sugar is fully incorporated with the vinegar then combine in: cilantro, jalapenos, and cucumbers.
6. Top everything with some peanuts.
7. Enjoy.

Classical Peanut Sauce II

Prep Time: 15 mins
Total Time: 15 mins

Servings per Recipe: 16
Calories   160 kcal
Fat   13.7 g
Carbohydrates 5.7g
Protein   6.5 g
Cholesterol   0 mg
Sodium   373 mg

Ingredients

- 1 1/2 C. creamy peanut butter
- 1/2 C. coconut milk
- 3 tbsps water
- 3 tbsps fresh lime juice
- 3 tbsps soy sauce
- 1 tbsp fish sauce
- 1 tbsp hot sauce
- 1 tbsp minced fresh ginger root
- 3 cloves garlic, minced
- 1/4 C. chopped fresh cilantro

Directions

1. Get a bowl, combine: garlic, peanut butter, ginger, coconut milk, hot sauce, water, fish sauce, lime juice, and soy sauce.
2. Stir the mix until it is smooth then add in the cilantro and stir everything again.
3. Enjoy.

THAI MANGO
Curry Chicken and Rice

🥣 Prep Time: 10 mins
⏱ Total Time: 55 mins

Servings per Recipe: 6
Calories   669 kcal
Fat   26.3 g
Carbohydrates   90.5g
Protein   22.6 g
Cholesterol   32 mg
Sodium   1785 mg

Ingredients

3 C. water
1 1/2 C. jasmine rice
1 tsp salt
3 skinless, boneless chicken breast halves
1/2 C. soy sauce
1 tbsp water, or as desired
1 (14 oz.) can coconut milk
1 C. white sugar
2 tbsps curry powder

1 mango - peeled, seeded, and diced
2 C. clover sprouts, or to taste
1 C. finely chopped cashews
1 bunch fresh cilantro, finely chopped
4 green onions, chopped

Directions

1. Get your rice boiling in water with some salt.
2. Once the mix is boiling set the heat to low, place a lid on the pot, and let the rice cook for 17 mins.
3. Now shut the heat and let everything stand for 7 mins.
4. Over heat, in a separate pot, combine your soy sauce, chicken, and 1 tbsp of water.
5. Place a lid on the pot and let the chicken cook for 22 mins.
6. Flip the chicken a few times so it cooks evenly then dice the meat into cubes.
7. Now get the following boiling in a separate pot: curry powder, coconut milk, and sugar.
8. Once the mix is boiling set the heat to low, add in the mango, and let the mix gently simmer for 7 mins.
9. Place you rice in a serving dish, and layer the following over each serving: chicken, sprouts, green onions, cashews, and cilantro.
10. Top everything with your curry sauce.
11. Enjoy.

Vietnamese Spring Rolls

Prep Time: 45 mins
Total Time: 50 mins

Servings per Recipe: 8	
Calories	82 kcal
Carbohydrates	15.8 g
Cholesterol	11 mg
Fat	0.7 g
Fiber	0.6 g
Protein	3.3 g
Sodium	305 mg

Ingredients

- 2 ounces rice vermicelli
- 8 rice wrappers (8.5 inch diameter)
- 8 large cooked shrimp - peeled, deveined and cut in half
- 1 1/3 tbsps chopped fresh Thai basil
- 3 tbsps chopped fresh mint leaves
- 3 tbsps chopped fresh cilantro
- 2 leaves lettuce, chopped
- 4 tsps fish sauce
- 1/4 cup water
- 2 tbsps fresh lime juice
- 1 clove garlic, minced
- 2 tbsps white sugar
- 1/2 tsp garlic chili sauce
- 3 tbsps hoisin sauce
- 1 tsp finely chopped peanuts

Directions

1. Cook rice vermicelli in boiling water for five minutes or until done and then drain.
2. Dip a rice wrapper in hot water for one second to soften it up before placing shrimp halves, basil, mint, vermicelli, cilantro and lettuce, and then roll this wrapper around these things.
3. Mix fish sauce, lime juice, garlic, water, sugar and chili sauce in a small bowl before mixing peanuts and hoisin sauce in a separate bowl.
4. Serve spring roll with these two sauces.

SPICY THAI Cabbage and Shrimp

Prep Time: 25 mins
Total Time: 35 mins

Servings per Recipe: 1
Calories 406 kcal
Fat 35.6 g
Carbohydrates 12.1g
Protein 12.3 g
Cholesterol 85 mg
Sodium 1017 mg

Ingredients

2 1/2 tbsps vegetable oil
1/4 C. water
1 C. shredded cabbage
1 tbsp minced garlic
8 large fresh shrimp, peeled and deveined
2 tsps crushed red pepper flakes
2 tbsps sliced onion
1 tbsp chopped fresh cilantro
1 tbsp soy sauce

Directions

1. Begin to stir fry your cabbage with 1 tbsp of water in 1 tbsp of oil for 1 mins.
2. Now place the cabbage to the side.
3. Add in 1.5 tbsp of oil to the pan and begin to stir fry your shrimp and garlic until the fish is fully cooked.
4. Now combine in the rest of the water, pepper, soy sauce, onion, and cilantro.
5. Let the mix fry for half a min then add in the cabbage and get everything hot again.
6. Enjoy.

Classical Pad Thai Noodle III

⏲ Prep Time: 30 mins
⏱ Total Time: 30 mins

Servings per Recipe: 4
Calories   452 kcal
Fat   28.6 g
Carbohydrates   45.8g
Protein   13.7 g
Cholesterol   0 mg
Sodium   478 mg

Ingredients

- 2 zucchini, ends trimmed
- 2 carrots
- 1 head red cabbage, thinly sliced
- 1 red bell pepper, thinly sliced
- 1/2 C. bean sprouts
- 3/4 C. raw almond butter
- 2 oranges, juiced
- 2 tbsps raw honey
- 1 tbsp minced fresh ginger root
- 1 tbsp Nama Shoyu (raw soy sauce)
- 1 tbsp unpasteurized miso
- 1 clove garlic, minced
- 1/4 tsp cayenne pepper

Directions

1. Grab a veggie peeler and cut your zucchini lengthwise.
2. Continue cutting the veggies into long streaks to create ribbons.
3. Create the same type of ribbons with your carrots.
4. Now get a bowl, combine: bean sprouts, carrots, bell peppers, and cabbage.
5. Stir the mix to evenly combine everything.
6. Get a 2nd bowl, combine: cayenne, almond butter, orange juice, garlic, miso, honey, Nama Shoyu, and ginger.
7. Add half of the 2nd bowl to the first bowl and stir the mix to evenly coat the veggies.
8. Add your zucchini to the bowl with the cabbage then top the zucchini with the rest of the sauce.
9. Stir everything to evenly distribute the zucchini throughout.
10. Enjoy.

VIETNAMESE Chicken Meatballs

Prep Time: 20 mins
Total Time: 55 mins

Servings per Recipe: 6
Calories   184 kcal
Carbohydrates   4.1 g
Cholesterol   69 mg
Fat   5.9 g
Fiber   0.1 g
Protein   26.5 g
Sodium   497 mg

Ingredients
1 1/2 pounds ground chicken
1 clove garlic, minced
1 egg white
1 tbsp rice wine
2 tbsps soy sauce
1/2 tsp Worcestershire sauce
2 tsps fish sauce
1/2 tsp white sugar
salt and white pepper to taste
2 tbsps cornstarch

1 tbsp sesame oil

Directions
1. Preheat the broiler of your oven before doing anything else.
2. Combine ground chicken, Worcestershire sauce, sugar, garlic, rice wine, soy sauce, egg white, fish sauce, salt, pepper, corn starch and sesame oil in a medium sized bowl before forming small balls out of it and threading them onto skewers.
3. Put these skewers on a baking sheet.
4. Broil it for 20 minutes or until you see that it is cooked.

Vietnamese Lamb Chops

Prep Time: 10 mins
Total Time: 8 hrs 30 mins

Servings per Recipe: 5
Calories   555 kcal
Carbohydrates   7.4 g
Cholesterol   151 mg
Fat   40.4 g
Fiber   0.6 g
Protein   38.6 g
Sodium   301 mg

Ingredients

15 (3 ounce) lamb loin chops (1-inch thick) lamb loin chops (1-inch thick)
2 cloves garlic, sliced
1 tsp garlic powder, or to taste
1 pinch chili powder
2 tbsps white sugar
freshly ground black pepper to taste
1 tbsp fresh lime juice

1 tbsp soy sauce
2 tbsps olive oil
1/4 cup chopped fresh cilantro
2 lime wedges
2 lemon wedges

Directions

1. Set your oven at 400 degrees F before doing anything else.
2. Add the garlic, garlic powder, sugar, salt, lime juice, chili powder, soy sauce, olive oil and pepper in a roasting pan over lamb chops.
3. Bake this in the preheated oven for about 30 minutes or until tender before garnishing it with cilantro and adding some lime juice.
4. Serve.

VIETNAMESE
Chicken Salad

Prep Time: 30 mins
Total Time: 30 mins

Servings per Recipe: 4
Calories 303 kcal
Carbohydrates 19.3 g
Cholesterol 37 mg
Fat 17.9 g
Fiber 5.7 g
Protein 19.2 g
Sodium 991 mg

Ingredients

- 1 tbsp finely chopped green chile peppers
- 1 tbsp rice vinegar
- 2 tbsps fresh lime juice
- 3 tbsps Asian fish sauce
- 3 cloves garlic, minced
- 1 tbsp white sugar
- 1 tbsp Asian (toasted) sesame oil
- 2 tbsps vegetable oil
- 1 tsp black pepper
- 2 cooked skinless boneless chicken breast halves, shredded
- 1/2 head cabbage, cored and thinly sliced
- 1 carrot, cut into matchsticks
- 1/3 onion, finely chopped
- 1/3 cup finely chopped dry roasted peanuts
- 1/3 cup chopped fresh cilantro

Directions

1. Combine chopped green chilies, sesame oil, lime juice, fish sauce, garlic, sugar, rice vinegar, vegetable oil and black pepper in a medium sized bowl very thoroughly so that the sugar is completely dissolved.
2. Mix chicken, carrot, onion, peanuts, cabbage and cilantro in a separate bowl.
3. Pour the bowl containing dressing over this and serve it after thoroughly mixing it.

Vietnamese Stir Fry

Prep Time: 20 mins
Total Time: 2 hrs 50 mins

Servings per Recipe: 5
Calories   475 kcal
Carbohydrates   8.8 g
Cholesterol   101 mg
Fat   34.4 g
Fiber   2 g
Protein   31.7 g
Sodium   1174 mg

Ingredients

- 1/4 cup olive oil
- 4 cloves garlic, minced
- 1 (1 inch) piece fresh ginger root, minced
- 1/4 cup fish sauce
- 1/4 cup reduced-sodium soy sauce
- 1 dash sesame oil
- 2 pounds sirloin tip, thinly sliced
- 1 tbsp vegetable oil
- 2 cloves garlic, minced
- 3 green onions, cut into 2 inch pieces
- 1 large onion, thinly sliced
- 2 cups frozen whole green beans, partially thawed
- 1/2 cup reduced-sodium beef broth
- 2 tbsps lime juice
- 1 tbsp chopped fresh Thai basil
- 1 tbsp chopped fresh mint
- 1 pinch red pepper flakes, or to taste
- 1/2 tsp ground black pepper
- 1/4 cup chopped fresh cilantro

Directions

1. Add a mixture of olive oil, ginger, fish sauce, 4 cloves of garlic, soy sauce, and sesame oil into a plastic bag containing beef sirloin tips and shake it well to get beef coated with the mixture.
2. Refrigerate it for at least two straight hours before removing the beef from the marinade.
3. Cook this beef in hot oil for about seven minutes or until you see that it is no longer pink before setting it aside on a plate.
4. Turn down the heat to medium and cook garlic, onion and green onion for about five minutes before adding green beans, lime juice, basil, mint, beef broth, red pepper flakes, pepper and also the beef.
5. Mix it thoroughly before adding cilantro.

VIETNAMESE
Tofu Pho

Prep Time: 15 mins
Total Time: 25 mins

Servings per Recipe: 4
Calories   159 kcal
Carbohydrates   29.2 g
Cholesterol   5 mg
Fat   2.3 g
Fiber   1.7 g
Protein   5.2 g
Sodium   991 mg

Ingredients

2 (14.5 ounce) cans chicken broth
2 star anise pods, or more to taste
3/4 tbsp ginger paste
1 tsp sriracha hot sauce, or more to taste
4 ounces tofu, cubed
1/2 cup broccoli florets
1/2 cup sliced mushrooms
1/4 cup chopped carrots
1/2 (8 ounce) package dried thin rice noodles
1 tbsp chopped green onion

Directions

1. Bring the mixture of chicken broth, ginger paste, star anise and sriracha hot sauce to boil before adding carrots, tofu, mushrooms and broccoli, and cooking it for seven minutes or until you see that the vegetables are tender.
2. Put noodles in hot water for about four minutes and drain.
3. After removing star anise from the broth mixture, add this mixture on top of noodles in serving bowls.
4. Serve.

Vietnamese Tofu Salad

🍲 Prep Time: 20 mins
🕒 Total Time: 1 hr 50 mins

Servings per Recipe: 6
Calories	200 kcal
Carbohydrates	18.4 g
Cholesterol	0 mg
Fat	11.7 g
Fiber	2.6 g
Protein	9.5 g
Sodium	636 mg

Ingredients

- 1 tbsp vegetable oil
- 2 tbsps chopped garlic
- 1 (14 ounce) package tofu, drained and cubed
- 1/2 cup peanuts
- 2 tbsps soy sauce
- 2 large cucumbers, peeled and thinly sliced
- 1/2 cup Vietnamese sweet chili sauce
- 1/4 cup lime juice
- 1 bunch chopped cilantro leaves

Directions

1. Cook garlic in hot oil for about thirty seconds before adding tofu and peanuts, and cooking it again until tofu is lightly brown.
2. Now add soy sauce and cook until you see that it is completely absorbed before refrigerating it for at least one hour.
3. In the mixture of chili sauce, cilantro, sliced cucumbers and lime juice add tofu, and mix it thoroughly before serving.
4. Enjoy.

VIETNAMESE
Shrimp Soup

Prep Time: 15 mins
Total Time: 40 mins

Servings per Recipe: 6
Calories	212 kcal
Carbohydrates	28.6 g
Cholesterol	52 mg
Fat	4.7 g
Fiber	2.7 g
Protein	14.4 g
Sodium	1156 mg

Ingredients

- 1 tbsp vegetable oil
- 2 tsps minced fresh garlic
- 2 tsps minced fresh ginger root
- 1 (10 ounce) package frozen chopped spinach, thawed and drained
- salt and black pepper to taste
- 2 quarts chicken stock
- 1 cup shrimp stock
- 1 tsp hot pepper sauce(optional)
- 1 tsp hoisin sauce(optional)
- 20 peeled and deveined medium shrimp
- 1 (6.75 ounce) package long rice noodles (rice vermicelli)
- 2 green onions, chopped(optional)

Directions

1. Cook garlic and ginger for about one minute before adding spinach, pepper and salt, and cooking it for 3 more minutes to get the spinach tender.
2. Add chicken stock, hoisin sauce, shrimp stock and hot pepper sauce, and cook this for a few more minutes.
3. In the end, add noodles and shrimp into it, and cook it for 4 minutes before adding green onions cooking it for another five minutes.
4. Add salt and pepper according to your taste before serving.
5. Enjoy.

Vietnamese Rice Noodle Salad

Prep Time: 15 mins
Total Time: 15 mins

Servings per Recipe: 4
Calories   432 kcal
Carbohydrates   89.5 g
Cholesterol   0 mg
Fat   5.3 g
Fiber   4.1 g
Protein   6.6 g
Sodium   188 mg

Ingredients

- 5 cloves garlic
- 1 cup loosely packed chopped cilantro
- 1/2 jalapeno pepper, seeded and minced
- 3 tbsps white sugar
- 1/4 cup fresh lime juice
- 3 tbsps vegetarian fish sauce
- 1 (12 ounce) package dried rice noodles
- 2 carrots, julienned
- 1 cucumber, halved lengthwise and chopped
- 1/4 cup chopped fresh mint
- 4 leaves napa cabbage
- 1/4 cup unsalted peanuts
- 4 sprigs fresh mint

Directions

1. Add a mashed mixture of hot pepper, garlic and cilantro into the bowl containing mixture of lime juice, sugar and fish sauce before letting it stand for at least five minutes.
2. Cook rice noodles in boiling salty water for two minutes before draining it and passing it through cold water to stop the process of cooking.
3. Mix sauce, carrots, cucumber, noodles, mint and Napa in large sized serving bowl very thoroughly before garnishing it with peanuts and mint sprigs.

VIETNAMESE
Beef Lettuce

🍲 Prep Time: 15 mins
🕐 Total Time: 1 hr

Servings per Recipe: 6
Calories   529 kcal
Carbohydrates   56.9 g
Cholesterol   69 mg
Fat   21 g
Fiber   4 g
Protein   26.3 g
Sodium   1481 mg

Ingredients

1 cup uncooked long grain white rice
2 cups water
5 tsps white sugar
1 clove garlic, minced
1/4 cup fish sauce
5 tbsps water
1 1/2 tbsps chili sauce
1 lemon, juiced
2 tbsps vegetable oil
3 cloves garlic, minced

1 pound ground beef
1 tbsp ground cumin
1 (28 ounce) can canned diced tomatoes
2 cups lettuce leaves, torn into 1/2 inch wide strips

Directions

1. Bring the water containing rice to boil before turning down the heat to low and cooking for 25 minutes.
2. Add mashed sugar and garlic to the mixture of chili sauce, fish sauce, lemon juice and water in a medium sized bowl.
3. Cook garlic in hot oil before adding beef and cumin, and cooking all this until you see that it is brown.
4. Now add half of that fish sauce mixture and tomatoes into the pan, and after turning down the heat to low, cook all this for twenty more minutes.
5. Add lettuce into this beef mixture before serving this over the cooked rice along with that remaining fish sauce.

Vietnamese Beef Pho

Prep Time: 10 mins
Total Time: 1 hr 30 mins

Servings per Recipe: 6
Calories	528 kcal
Carbohydrates	73.1 g
Cholesterol	51 mg
Fat	13.6 g
Fiber	3.9 g
Protein	27.1 g
Sodium	2844 mg

Ingredients

- 4 quarts beef broth
- 1 large onion, sliced into rings
- 6 slices fresh ginger root
- 1 lemon grass
- 1 cinnamon stick
- 1 tsp whole black peppercorns
- 1 pound sirloin tip, cut into thin slices
- 1/2 pound bean sprouts
- 1 cup fresh basil leaves
- 1 cup fresh mint leaves
- 1 cup loosely packed cilantro leaves
- 3 fresh jalapeno peppers, sliced into rings
- 2 limes, cut into wedges
- 2 (8 ounce) packages dried rice noodles
- 1/2 tbsp hoisin sauce
- 1 dash hot pepper sauce
- 3 tbsps fish sauce

Directions

1. Bring the mixture of broth, onion, lemon grass, cinnamon, ginger and peppercorns to boil before turning down the heat to low and cooking it for about one hour.
2. Place bean sprouts, basil, cilantro, chilies, mint and lime on a platter very neatly.
3. Place noodles in hot water for about 15 minutes before placing it in six different bowls evenly.
4. Put raw beef over it before pouring in hot broth.
5. Serve it with the platter and sauces.

VIETNAMESE
Chicken Wings

🥣 Prep Time: 15 mins
⏱ Total Time: 2 hrs 45 mins

Servings per Recipe: 4
Calories   716 kcal
Carbohydrates   9.1 g
Cholesterol   213 mg
Fat   50.9 g
Fiber   0.8 g
Protein   53 g
Sodium   2781 mg

Ingredients

12 chicken wings, tips removed and wings cut in half at joint
2 cloves garlic, peeled and coarsely chopped
1/2 onion, cut into chunks
1/4 cup soy sauce
1/4 cup Asian fish sauce
2 tbsps fresh lemon juice
2 tbsps sesame oil
1 tsp salt
1 tsp freshly ground black pepper
1 tbsp garlic powder
1 tbsp white sugar

Directions

1. Into the mixture of chicken wings, onion and garlic in large sized bowl; add fish sauce, sesame oi, salt, sugar, garlic powder, pepper and lemon juice before refrigerating it covered for at least two hours.
2. Preheat your oven at 400 degrees F and place aluminum foil in the baking dish.
3. Reserving some marinade for brushing; place all the wings on the baking dish and bake it for about 30 minutes or until you see that these have turned golden brown.

Vietnamese Chutney

Prep Time: 15 mins
Total Time: 15 mins

Servings per Recipe: 5	
Calories	15 kcal
Carbohydrates	3.7 g
Cholesterol	0 mg
Fat	0 g
Fiber	0.3 g
Protein	0.4 g
Sodium	220 mg

Ingredients

1/4 cup white sugar
1/2 cup warm water
1/4 cup fish sauce
1/3 cup distilled white vinegar
1/2 lemon, juiced
3 cloves garlic, minced
3 Thai chile peppers, chopped
1 green onion, thinly sliced

Directions

1. In a mixture of warm water and sugar; add fish sauce, garlic, green onion, lemon juice, vinegar and chili pepper.
2. Mix all this very thoroughly before serving.
3. Enjoy.

NOTE: Use this condiment for dipping spring rolls in, or as a topping for jasmine rice.

VIETNAMESE
Chicken & Curry Soup

Prep Time: 30 mins
Total Time: 2 hrs 45 mins

Servings per Recipe: 8
Calories   512 kcal
Carbohydrates   40.6 g
Cholesterol   75 mg
Fat   26.8 g
Fiber   6.7 g
Protein   29.8 g
Sodium   374 mg

Ingredients
2 tbsps vegetable oil
1 (3 pound) whole chicken, skin removed and cut into pieces
1 onion, cut into chunks
2 shallots, thinly sliced
2 cloves garlic, chopped
1/8 cup thinly sliced fresh ginger root
1 stalk lemon grass, cut into 2 inch pieces
4 tbsps curry powder
1 green bell pepper, cut into 1 inch pieces
2 carrots, sliced diagonally
1 quart chicken broth
1 quart water
2 tbsps fish sauce
2 kaffir lime leaves
1 bay leaf
2 tsps red pepper flakes
8 small potatoes, quartered
1 (14 ounce) can coconut milk
1 bunch fresh cilantro

Directions
1. Cook onion and chicken in hot oil until you see that onions are soft and then set it aside for later use.
2. Cook shallots in the same pan for one minute before adding garlic, lemon grass, ginger and curry powder, and cooking it for another five minutes.
3. Add pepper and carrots before stirring in chicken, onion, fish sauce, chicken broth and water.
4. Also add lime leaves, red pepper flakes and bay leaf before bringing all this to boil and adding potatoes.
5. Add coconut milk and cook it for 60 minutes after turning down the heat to low.
6. Garnish with a sprig of fresh cilantro.
7. Serve.

Lemon Grass Chicken

Prep Time: 15 mins
Total Time: 40 mins

Servings per Recipe: 4
Calories	813 kcal
Carbohydrates	4.6 g
Cholesterol	255 mg
Fat	58.4 g
Fiber	0.8 g
Protein	63.8 g
Sodium	515 mg

Ingredients

- 2 tbsps vegetable oil
- 1 lemon grass, minced
- 1 (3 pound) whole chicken, cut into pieces
- 2/3 cup water
- 1 tbsp fish sauce
- 1 1/2 tbsps curry powder
- 1 tbsp cornstarch
- 1 tbsp chopped cilantro (optional)

Directions

1. Cook lemon grass in hot oil for about 5 minutes before adding chicken and cooking it until you see that the chicken is no longer pink from the center.
2. Now add fish sauce, curry powder and water into the pan before turning the heat up to high and cooking it for another 15 minutes.
3. Now add the mixture of curry sauce and cornstarch into the pan, and cook all this for another five minutes.
4. Garnish with cilantro before serving.

LA SA GA
Vietnamese Pasta Soup

Prep Time: 20 mins
Total Time: 45 mins

Servings per Recipe: 8
Calories 333 kcal
Carbohydrates 41.8 g
Cholesterol 15 mg
Fat 13.5 g
Fiber 3.1 g
Protein 15.1 g
Sodium 1710 mg

Ingredients

3 tbsps peanut oil
1 cup diced onion
3 tbsps minced garlic
1 cup coconut milk, divided
1 tbsp red curry paste, or more to taste
2 cooked chicken breast halves, shredded
8 cups chicken stock
6 tbsps soy sauce, or to taste
1/4 cup fish sauce, or to taste
1 1/2 pounds angel hair pasta
1/4 cup chopped fresh basil, or to taste

Directions

1. Cook onion and garlic in hot oil for about four minutes before adding coconut milk and stirring it continuously for about two minutes.
2. Now add curry paste and stir it well for about two more minutes.
3. Introduce chicken stock into the pan and cook it for about four minutes after turning up the heat to medium.
4. Cook it for another four minutes after adding the remaining coconut milk.
5. Stir in angel hair pasta before covering up the pot and cooking it for ten more minutes.
6. Add basil before serving.

Vietnamese Coffee

Prep Time: 5 mins
Total Time: 10 mins

Servings per Recipe: 4
Calories   129 kcal
Fat   3.3 g
Carbohydrates   22g
Protein   3.3 g
Cholesterol   13 mg
Sodium   64 mg

Ingredients

4 C. water
1/2 C. dark roast ground coffee beans
1/2 C. sweetened condensed milk
16 ice cubes

Directions

1. Make your coffee with the 4 C. of fresh water. Then add 2 tbsps of condensed milk.
2. Serve the coffee hot and pour it over 4 ices cubes in a glass.
3. Enjoy.

SOUTHEAST ASIAN
Rice Noodle Pesto

🥘 Prep Time: 30 mins
🕐 Total Time: 45 mins

Servings per Recipe: 4
Calories   694 kcal
Fat   29.8 g
Carbohydrates   98.8g
Protein   6.8 g
Cholesterol   0 mg
Sodium   217 mg

Ingredients

- 1 lb dried rice noodles
- 1 1/2 C. chopped fresh cilantro
- 1/2 C. sweet Thai basil
- 2 cloves garlic, halved
- 1/2 tsp minced lemon grass bulb
- 1 jalapeno pepper, seeded and minced
- 1 tbsp vegetarian fish sauce
- 4 tbsps chopped, unsalted dry-roasted peanuts
- 7 tbsps canola oil
- 1/2 lime, cut into wedges
- salt and pepper to taste

Directions

1. Let your noodles sit submerged in water for 40 mins then remove all the liquids.
2. Add the following to the bowl of food processor and begin to puree: 2 tbsps peanuts, cilantro, fish sauce, basil, jalapenos, garlic cloves, and lemongrass.
3. Now add in your oil and continue pulsing for a min then add the rest of the peanuts.
4. Now heat your noodles in 1/2 C. of water until all the water has been absorbed by the noodles.
5. Pour in your most of basil puree then stir everything. Taste the mix then add the rest of the puree if you prefer.
6. Top the pasta with 2 more tbsp of peanuts.
7. Enjoy.

Vietnamese Vegetarian Curry Soup

Prep Time: 30 mins
Total Time: 2 hrs

Servings per Recipe: 8
Calories   479 kcal
Fat   26.5 g
Carbohydrates   51.4g
Protein   16.4 g
Cholesterol   0 mg
Sodium   271 mg

Ingredients

- 2 tbsps vegetable oil
- 1 onion, coarsely chopped
- 2 shallots, thinly sliced
- 2 cloves garlic, chopped
- 2 inch piece fresh ginger root, thinly sliced
- 1 stalk lemon grass, cut into 2 inch pieces
- 4 tbsps curry powder
- 1 green bell pepper, coarsely chopped
- 2 carrots, peeled and diagonally sliced
- 8 mushrooms, sliced
- 1 lb fried tofu, cut into bite-size pieces
- 4 C. vegetable broth
- 4 C. water
- 2 tbsps vegetarian fish sauce (optional)
- 2 tsps red pepper flakes
- 1 bay leaf
- 2 kaffir lime leaves
- 8 small potatoes, quartered
- 1 (14 oz.) can coconut milk
- 2 C. fresh bean sprouts, for garnish
- 8 sprigs fresh chopped cilantro, for garnish

Directions

1. Stir fry your shallots and onions in oil until the onions are see through then add in the curry powder, garlic, lemon grass, and ginger.
2. Let the mix continue to fry for 6 mins then add the tofu, green pepper, mushrooms, and carrots.
3. Stir the mix then add in the water, pepper flakes, fish sauce, and veggie stock.
4. Get everything boiling then add the coconut milk and the potatoes.
5. Get the mix boiling again then set the heat to low and let the mix gently boil for 50 mins.
6. When serving the dish top each serving with cilantro and bean sprouts.
7. Enjoy.

BO NUONG XA
Mint and Basil Beef

Prep Time: 30 mins
Total Time: 4 hrs 45 mins

Servings per Recipe: 6
Calories   204 kcal
Fat   11.1 g
Carbohydrates   5.7g
Protein   20.1 g
Cholesterol   61 mg
Sodium   348 mg

Ingredients

2 tsps white sugar
2 tbsps soy sauce
1 tsp ground black pepper
2 cloves garlic, minced
2 stalks lemon grass, minced
2 tsps sesame seeds
1 1/2 lbs sirloin tip, thinly sliced
skewers
12 leaves romaine lettuce
fresh cilantro for garnish
fresh basil for garnish
fresh mint for garnish
thinly sliced green onion for garnish

Directions

1. Get a bowl, combine: sesame seeds, sugar, lemon grass, soy sauce, garlic, and pepper. Add in the meat and stir the mix.
2. Place a covering of plastic on the bowl and put everything in the fridge for 5 hrs.
3. Now get your grill hot and stake your meat onto the skewers. Grill the kebabs for 6 mins per side.
4. When serving the dish place the meat on some fresh lettuce leaves then top everything with green onions, cilantro, basil, and mint.
5. Enjoy.

Vietnamese Bean and Beef Stir Fry

Prep Time: 10 mins
Total Time: 30 mins

Servings per Recipe: 4
Calories   375 kcal
Fat   28.6 g
Carbohydrates   6.2g
Protein   23 g
Cholesterol   76 mg
Sodium   139 mg

Ingredients

1 clove garlic, minced
1/4 tsp ground black pepper
1 tsp cornstarch
1 tsp vegetable oil
1 lb sirloin tips, thinly sliced
3 tbsps vegetable oil
1/2 onion, thinly sliced

2 C. fresh green beans, washed and trimmed
1/4 C. chicken broth
1 tsp soy sauce

Directions

1. Get a bowl, combine: 1 tsp veggie oil, garlic, cornstarch, and black pepper. Combine in the beef then stir the mix again.
2. Add 2 more tsp of oil to a wok and get it hot. Once the oil is hot begin to stir the meat for 3 mins then place the meat to the side.
3. Add 1 more tsp to the wok and being to stir your onions until they are soft then add in the broth, and green beans.
4. Place a lid on the wok if possible then let the mix simmer for 6 mins. Add in the beef and soy sauce and cook the mix for 3 more mins.
5. Enjoy.

VIETNAMESE
Chicken Pho

Prep Time: 10 mins
Total Time: 45 mins

Servings per Recipe: 2
Calories	521 kcal
Fat	13.7 g
Carbohydrates	54.4g
Protein	49.8 g
Cholesterol	1107 mg
Sodium	3270 mg

Ingredients

4 oz. dry Chinese egg noodles
6 C. chicken stock
2 tbsps fish sauce
4 cloves garlic, minced
2 tsps minced fresh ginger root
1 tbsp minced lemon grass
5 green onions, chopped
2 C. cubed cooked chicken
1 C. bean sprouts
1 C. chopped bok choy

Directions

1. Get a big pot of water boiling then combine in the noodles and cook them for 9 mins. Then remove the liquids and place the noodles to the side.
2. Now add the following to the same pot and get it all boiling again: green onions, chickens tock, lemon grass, fish sauce, ginger, and garlic.
3. Once the mix is boiling set the heat to low and let everything gently cook for 12 mins.
4. Combine in the bok choy, bean sprouts, and chicken.
5. Continue simmering the mix for 7 mins.
6. Divide the noodles into two bowls for serving then top them liberally with the soup.
7. Enjoy.

Vietnamese Bamboo Tofu

🥣 Prep Time: 20 mins
🕐 Total Time: 40 mins

Servings per Recipe: 4
Calories   380 kcal
Fat   21.6 g
Carbohydrates   28.2g
Protein   11.7 g
Cholesterol   0 mg
Sodium   796 mg

Ingredients

- 2 tbsps white sugar
- 3 tbsps soy sauce
- 1 C. dry white wine
- 1/2 C. chicken broth
- 1 (14 oz.) package tofu, drained
- salt and pepper to taste
- 1 tbsp cornstarch
- 3 C. oil for frying, or as needed
- 1 onion, chopped
- 4 plum tomatoes, sliced into thin wedges
- 12 oz. fresh green beans, trimmed and cut into 3 inch pieces
- 1 C. bamboo shoots, drained and sliced
- 1 C. chicken broth, or as needed
- 2 tbsps cornstarch
- 3 tbsps water

Directions

1. Get a bowl, combine: 1/2 C. broth, white sugar, white wine, and soy sauce.
2. Drain and dry your tofu then dice it into cubes. Top the tofu with some pepper and salt then coat everything with 1 tbsp of cornstarch.
3. Get about 1 in. of oil hot in a wok then deep fry the tofu in the oil until it is golden.
4. Place the tofu to the side on some paper towels.
5. In a 2nd frying pan get 1 tbsp of oil hot then begin to stir fry your green beans and onions for 6 mins then add some pepper and salt.
6. Add in your tomatoes and cook them for 5 mins then add the bamboo shoots.
7. Now combine in the sauce and beans and get everything boiling.
8. Let the mix boil for 7 mins while stirring. Add some more broth (1 C.) if all the liquid cooks out.
9. Combine in the rest of the cornstarch (2 tbsp) with water until smooth then add it to the mix.
10. Stir and simmer everything until the mix is thick then add the tofu.
11. Enjoy.

VIETNAMESE
Vermicelli

🥣 Prep Time: 35 mins
🕐 Total Time: 1 hr

Servings per Recipe: 2
Calories   659 kcal
Fat   12.8 g
Carbohydrates   112.3g
Protein   26.2 g
Cholesterol   36 mg
Sodium   2565 mg

Ingredients

- 1/4 C. white vinegar
- 1/4 C. fish sauce
- 2 tbsps white sugar
- 2 tbsps lime juice
- 1 clove garlic, minced
- 1/4 tsp red pepper flakes
- 1/2 tsp canola oil
- 2 tbsps chopped shallots
- 2 skewers
- 8 medium shrimp, with shells
- 1 (8 oz.) package rice vermicelli noodles
- 1 C. finely chopped lettuce
- 1 C. bean sprouts
- 1 English cucumber, cut into 2-inch matchsticks
- 1/4 C. finely chopped pickled carrots
- 1/4 C. finely chopped diakon radish
- 3 tbsps chopped cilantro
- 3 tbsps finely chopped Thai basil
- 3 tbsps chopped fresh mint
- 1/4 C. crushed peanuts

Directions

1. Get a bowl, combine: pepper flakes, vinegar, garlic, fish sauce, lime juice, and sugar. Let this mix sit on the side.
2. Now begin to stir fry your shallots in veggie oil for 9 mins.
3. Get your grill hot and coat the grate with oil.
4. Stake 4 pieces of shrimp onto skewers then grill them for 3 mins per side. Then remove the shrimp from the grill.
5. Begin to boil your vermicelli in water for 13 mins then remove all the liquids and run the noodles under some cold water.
6. Evenly divide the following between serving bowls: shallots, vermicelli, lettuce, peanuts, bean sprouts, mint, Thai basil, cucumbers, cilantro, carrots, and daikon. Serve everything with a shrimp kabob and some of the lime sauce from the 1st bowl.
7. Add some sauce to the serving and stir it.
8. Enjoy.

Southeast Chicken Breast

Prep Time: 15 mins
Total Time: 30 mins

Servings per Recipe: 6
Calories   231 kcal
Fat   5.4 g
Carbohydrates   32g
Protein   13.5 g
Cholesterol   28 mg
Sodium   149 mg

Ingredients

- 1 tbsp vegetable oil
- 1 small yellow onion, chopped
- 1 (8 oz.) package baby bella mushrooms, chopped
- 4 cloves garlic, minced
- 8 C. water
- 1 (6.75 oz.) package rice stick noodles (such as Maifun(R))
- 8 tsps chicken bouillon
- 2 cooked chicken breasts, shredded
- 4 green onions, chopped
- 1/3 C. chopped fresh cilantro
- 2 C. bean sprouts
- 1 lime, sliced into wedges
- 1 dash Sriracha hot sauce, or more to taste

Directions

1. Stir fry your garlic, mushrooms, and onions for 8 mins then combine in the bouillon, noodles, and water.
2. Get everything boiling then set the heat to low.
3. Combine in the cilantro, green onions, and chicken.
4. Let the mix cook for 8 more mins then divide the soup between serving bowls.
5. When serving the soup top it with some sriracha, bean sprouts, and lime juice.
6. Enjoy.

VIETNAMESE
Sping Rolls II

🥣 Prep Time: 1 hr
🕒 Total Time: 1 hr 25 mins

Servings per Recipe: 12
Calories   132 kcal
Fat   5.2 g
Carbohydrates   14.4g
Protein   6.5 g
Cholesterol   45 mg
Sodium   225 mg

Ingredients

2 oz. dried thin rice noodles
3/4 C. ground chicken
1/4 C. shrimp - washed, peeled, and cut into small pieces
2 large eggs, beaten
1 carrot, grated
4 wood fungus mushrooms, chopped
2 green onions, chopped
1/2 tsp white sugar
1/2 tsp salt
1/2 tsp ground black pepper
24 rice paper wrappers
2 C. vegetable oil for frying

Directions

1. Let your noodles sit submerged in water for 30 mins then remove all the liquids and dice the noodles into 3 inch pieces.
2. Get a bowl, combine: green onions, noodles, mushrooms, chicken, carrots, shrimp, and eggs.
3. Add in the black pepper, salt, and sugar then stir the mix.
4. Submerge 1 wrapper in some water then layer 1 tbsp of mix in the middle.
5. Roll up the edges of the wrapper and tightly to form a nice spring roll.
6. Continue with the rest of the wrappers and ingredients.
7. Fry your rolls, 3 at a time, in oil for 6 mins until golden.
8. Enjoy.

Vietnamese Sandwiches

Prep Time: 20 mins
Total Time: 30 mins

Servings per Recipe: 6
Calories   388 kcal
Fat   3.3 g
Carbohydrates   60.9 g
Protein   28.2 g
Cholesterol   148 mg
Sodium   886 mg

Ingredients

1 large carrot, peeled and shredded
1 stalk celery, chopped
2 scallions (green onions), chopped
1/4 C. rice vinegar
1/3 C. chopped fresh cilantro
3 tbsps low-fat mayonnaise
3 tbsps low-fat plain yogurt
1 tbsp lime juice
1/8 tsp cayenne pepper

3 (12 inch) French baguettes, cut into halves
1 lb frozen cooked prawns, thawed and tails removed
18 thin slices cucumber, or more to taste

Directions

1. Get a bowl, combine: scallions, carrots, and celery. Top the mix with the vinegar and stir everything.
2. Now get a 2nd bowl, combine: cayenne, cilantro, lime juice, yogurt, and mayo.
3. Coat one side of your bread with 2 tbsp of mayo sauce then layer the veggies on top of the sauce.
4. Add the prawns to the rest of the yogurt mix and layer them on top of the veggies in the sandwich.
5. Add a final layer of cucumber then form a sandwich with the other piece of bread.
6. Cut the sandwich into 6 pieces and serve.
7. Enjoy.

VIETNAMESE Chicken and Rice Soup

🥣 Prep Time: 10 mins
🕐 Total Time: 2 hrs 25 mins

Servings per Recipe: 4
Calories   642 kcal
Fat   42.3 g
Carbohydrates   9.8g
Protein   53 g
Cholesterol   1210 mg
Sodium   1943 mg

Ingredients
1/8 C. uncooked jasmine rice
1 (2.5 lb) whole chicken
3 (2 inch) pieces fresh ginger root
1 stalk lemon grass, chopped
1 tbsp salt, or to taste
1/4 C. chopped cilantro
1/8 C. chopped fresh chives
ground black pepper to taste
1 lime, cut into 8 wedges

Directions
1. Get the following boiling in a large pot: salt, chicken, lemon grass, water, and ginger.
2. Once the mix is boiling place a lid on the pot, set the heat to low, and let the contents gently cook for 90 mins.
3. Now run the contents through a strainer and place the chicken to the side and the liquid back in the pot. Remove the bones and skin from the chicken and dice the meat into small pieces.
4. Add the rice to the broth and get everything boiling. Once the mix is boiling set the heat to medium and cook the mix for 35 mins.
5. Add the rice to a bowl and add the chicken, pepper, chives, and cilantro on top.
6. Cover everything with lime juice.
7. Enjoy.

Taiwanese Corn Soup

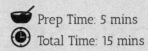
Prep Time: 5 mins
Total Time: 15 mins

Servings per Recipe: 4
Calories 121 kcal
Fat 1.9 g
Carbohydrates 24.1g
Protein 5 g
Cholesterol 48 mg
Sodium 409 mg

Ingredients
- (15 oz.) can cream style corn
- 1 (14.5 oz.) can low-sodium chicken broth
- 1 egg, beaten
- 1 tbsp cornstarch
- 2 tbsps water

Directions
1. Get the following boiling in a large pot: broth and cream corn.
2. Get a bowl, combine: water and cornstarch.
3. Mix the contents until smooth then add the mix with the boiling broth.
4. Let the broth continue to cook for 4 mins then add the whisked eggs slowly.
5. Stir the soup while adding in your eggs.
6. Enjoy.

BO LUC LAC
Garlic Sirloin w/ Vinaigrette

Prep Time: 30 mins
Total Time: 1 hr 35 mins

Servings per Recipe: 4
Calories   292 kcal
Fat   17.4 g
Carbohydrates   13.3 g
Protein   21.7 g
Cholesterol   60 mg
Sodium   1238 mg

Ingredients

Beef Marinade:
2 tbsps minced garlic
2 tbsps oyster sauce
1 1/2 tbsps white sugar
1 tbsp fish sauce
1 tbsp sesame oil
1 tbsp soy sauce
1 tsp hoisin sauce
1 1/2 lbs beef top sirloin, cut into 1-inch cubes
Vinaigrette:
1/2 C. rice vinegar
1 1/2 tbsps white sugar
1 1/2 tsps salt
1 red onion, thinly sliced
Dipping Sauce:
1 lime, juiced
1/2 tsp salt
1/2 tsp ground black pepper
2 tbsps cooking oil
2 bunches watercress, torn
2 tomatoes, thinly sliced

Directions

1. Get a bowl, combine: hoisin, garlic, soy sauce, oyster sauce, sesame oil, 1.5 tbsp sugar, and fish sauce.
2. Stir the mix until it is smooth then add in the beef. Stir the meat then place a covering of plastic on the bowl and put everything in the fridge for 60 mins.
3. Get a 2nd bowl, combine: onions, vinegar, 1.2 tsp salt, and 1.5 tbsp sugar.
4. Stir the mix until it is smooth then place it in the fridge for 13 mins.
5. Now get a 3rd bowl, combine: black pepper, lime juice, and 1/2 tsp salt. Place the sauce in some ramekins for dipping later.
6. Begin to stir your beef in hot oil, in a wok.
7. Brown the beef in batches for 3 mins then stir everything for 3 more mins until done.
8. Add a layer of watercress on a platter for serving then add the tomatoes, top the veggies with the vinaigrette.
9. Now add your beef and place the onions in 2nd bowl for serving over everything.
10. Enjoy with the ramekins of sauce.

Taiwanese Corn Soup II
(Creamy)

Prep Time: 10 mins
Total Time: 50 mins

Servings per Recipe: 6
Calories   157 kcal
Fat   3.3 g
Carbohydrates   16.2g
Protein   16 g
Cholesterol   26 mg
Sodium   1052 mg

Ingredients

- 1/2 lb skinless, boneless chicken breast meat - finely diced
- 1 tbsp sherry
- 1/4 tsp salt
- 2 egg whites
- 1 (14.75 oz.) can cream-style corn
- 4 C. chicken broth
- 2 tsps soy sauce
- 1/4 C. water
- 2 tbsps cornstarch
- 4 slices crisp cooked bacon, crumbled

Directions

1. Get a bowl, combine: chicken, egg whites, sherry, and salt.
2. Combine in the cream corn and continue mixing everything until it's smooth.
3. Now get the following boiling in a wok: soy sauce and chicken broth.
4. Combine in the chicken mix and get everything boiling again.
5. Now set the heat to low, and cook the soup for 5 mins while stirring.
6. Combine some cornstarch and water then pour this mix into your boiling soup and keep stirring everything for 3 more mins. Then add in your bacon and serve.
7. Enjoy.

EASY
Egg and Pea Soup

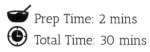
Prep Time: 2 mins
Total Time: 30 mins

Servings per Recipe: 6
Calories 35 kcal
Fat 1.9 g
Carbohydrates 2.5g
Protein < 2.4 g
Cholesterol 31 mg
Sodium 639 mg

Ingredients
4 C. seasoned chicken broth
1/2 C. frozen green peas
1 egg, beaten

Directions
1. Get your peas and broth boiling. Then once the mix is boiling add in your whisked eggs gradually to form ribbons.
2. Then add in your green onions and serve.
3. Enjoy.

Classical Egg Drop Soup

Prep Time: 10 mins
Total Time: 20 mins

Servings per Recipe: 6
Calories   62 kcal
Fat   2.8 g
Carbohydrates   4.7 g
Protein   4.5 g
Cholesterol   94 mg
Sodium   1872 mg

Ingredients

- 8 cubes chicken bouillon
- 6 C. hot water
- 2 tbsps cornstarch
- 2 tbsps soy sauce
- 3 tbsps distilled white vinegar
- 1 green onion, minced
- 3 eggs, beaten

Directions

1. Get a large pot and begin to heat some hot water and bouillon.
2. Stir and heat the mix until the bouillon is completely dissolved.
3. Now add in: the green onions, soy sauce, and vinegar.
4. Get the mix boiling then set the heat to low.
5. Slowly add in your whisked eggs while stirring.
6. Once the eggs have set, shut the heat.
7. Enjoy.

HOT AND SPICY Soup

🥣 Prep Time: 30 mins
🕐 Total Time: 1 hr

Servings per Recipe: 6
Calories   116 kcal
Fat   6.3 g
Carbohydrates   8.7g
Protein   7.4 g
Cholesterol   41 mg
Sodium   465 mg

Ingredients

- 5 dried wood ear mushrooms
- 4 dried shiitake mushrooms
- 8 dried tiger lily buds
- 4 C. chicken stock
- 1/3 C. diced bamboo shoots
- 1/3 C. lean ground pork
- 1 tsp soy sauce
- 1/2 tsp white sugar
- 1 tsp salt
- 1/2 tsp ground white pepper
- 2 tbsps red wine vinegar
- 2 tbsps cornstarch
- 3 tbsps water
- 1/2 (16 oz.) package firm tofu, cubed
- 1 egg, lightly beaten
- 1 tsp sesame oil
- 2 tbsps thinly sliced green onion

Directions

1. In warm water, for 30 mins, submerge your tiger lily and mushrooms, in a bowl.
2. Now remove any stems and cut the mushrooms and tiger lilly.
3. Now get the following boiling in a large pot: pork, mushrooms, bamboo shoots, tiger lily, and stock.
4. Let the mix cook for 12 mins then add: vinegar, soy sauce, white pepper, sugar, and salt.
5. Grab a small bowl, combine: some of the hot soup, 3 tbsps water, and cornstarch.
6. Mix everything until it's smooth then combine everything together and stir.
7. Get the mix completely boiling then add in the bean curds and cook the soup for 3 more mins.
8. Now shut the heat and slowly add in the eggs.
9. Let the eggs set then add the sesame oil and the scallions.
10. Enjoy.

Made in the USA
Monee, IL
17 May 2021